Church Dramas: Volume 1

Church Dramas: Volume 1

Comedies & Dramas for the Sunday Service

Rebecca Knill

Writers Club Press

San Jose New York Lincoln Shanghai

Church Dramas: Volume 1
Comedies & Dramas for the Sunday Service

Writers Club Press
an imprint of iUniverse, Inc.
For information address:
iUniverse, Inc.
5220 S. 16th St., Suite 200
Lincoln, NE 68512
www.iuniverse.com

Cover design by Marden Wright
Cover photo by Mark Salzwedel

ISBN: 0-595-19986-0

Printed in the United States of America

Use Of Material

The following scripts are copyrighted material and subject to royalty. Requests for use must be made in writing before rehearsal to rknill@aol.com. Additional information is available online at http://www.churchdramas.com.

To my parents

Contents

Acknowledgments

I would like to acknowledge and thank the following entities and individuals for their encouragement, inspiration, and support in compiling this book series: Mark Salzwedel, The Minneapolis Playwrights' Center, St. Peter's Church, The Catholic Appalachian Project, InterAct Theater, Wooddale Church, Patrice Blaeser, Karin Ederer, Mark Alan English, Ian Kennedy, Arthur Moore, Ann Marie Rodgers, Ewa Ushio, and Marden Wright.

Introduction

Most of the scripts contained in the *Church Dramas* books are categorized as "sermon enhancement dramas." Sermon enhancement dramas are designed to set up the subsequent teaching by:

- illustrating or providing entertainment related to the sermon topic;

- raising a question that will be answered in the sermon;

- providing background or supplementary information on the sermon topic or theme;

- evoking an emotion—such as anger or loneliness—to set the tone for the sermon.

Some of the dramas in this book do not mention God or religion. This is intentional. A sermon enhancement drama is not intended to stand on its own as a teaching. To be as accessible of a lead-in as possible, sermon enhancement dramas sometimes provide a parallel, secular storyline to better accommodate the widest audience. Scriptures noted at the top of each piece provide additional insight into the sermon topic but are not necessarily that upon which the drama is based.

In addition to sermon enhancements, other types of church dramas are:

- Christian Education, such as Sunday school classes. This type of drama is intended to stand on its own as a teaching.

- Outreach events, such as full-length plays or dinner theaters. These events are designed to introduce the church to community members in a low-key, non-threatening manner.

The Age Of Reason

THEME: Persistence.

DRAMA SUMMARY: A 75-year old mother persists in pursuing her dream of completing seminary school but encounters resistance from her daughter.

SCRIPTURAL REFERENCE: "You will keep in perfect peace him whose mind is steadfast, because he trusts in you. Trust in the Lord forever, for the Lord, the Lord, is the Rock eternal." *Isaiah 26:4.*

CHARACTERS:

GERDA, 75-ish

BARB, Gerda's adult daughter

SETTING: Kitchen Table

AUTHOR'S NOTES: *The Age of Reason* is, in part, about how adult children shoo their elderly parents to a waiting room to die. The character of the mother was written to honor my late next-door-neighbor, Gerda Ottoson. I was particularly fond of the real Gerda's feisty nature, and in this drama, while her desire to serve God was sincere, I believe the character of Gerda also enjoyed messing with her daughter's mind.

SCENE: GERDA sits at the kitchen table with a loan brochure, a pen, and several library books. There is a Bible on the table. BARB enters, carrying a bag of groceries.

BARB: Hi, Mom. *(She kisses her mother on the top of her head and spies the brochure.)* What's that?

GERDA: It's a loan application.

BARB: *(Sighing wearily, as she takes groceries out of the bag.)* Mom, we've talked about this.

GERDA: *(Hopefully.)* I can make the payments. I just need you to co-sign.

BARB: *(Defensively.)* It's not the money—although I can't let you throw it away like that either.

GERDA: *(Gently.)* I wouldn't be throwing it away, Barb. I'd be fulfilling my life's goal.

BARB: Four years at the Seminary is going to cost you at least $30,000. And what's the point of getting a degree, anyway? Are you planning to become a pastor?

GERDA: *(Confidently.)* I could.

BARB: *(Gently.)* You know I love you, Mom. But let's be realistic. Thirty thousand dollars!

GERDA: *(Repeating.)* I can make the payments.

BARB: *(With her hands on her hips, challenging GERDA.)* Over how many years?

GERDA: *(Shrugging.)* Thirty.

BARB: Well, how practical is *that?* *(GERDA looks at BARB, but doesn't say anything. BARB realizes her insensitivity and hastily backtracks.)* I mean, what if you need that money in the meantime? Why not play it safe?

GERDA: *(Earnestly.)* I've played it safe all my life. This is my chance to pursue my dream.

BARB: I just don't know why you're bothering. Wouldn't you rather spend your time doing something more meaningful?

GERDA: *(Confidently.)* I can't think of anything more meaningful than dedicating my life to God.

BARB: *(Grimly.)* Mom, at your age, dedicating your life to God is not quite the same thing.

GERDA: *(Earnestly.)* But I really believe that this is my calling.

BARB *(Exasperated.)* You're dreaming up these wild ideas! People are going to think you're becoming senile. And how would I even know if you were?

GERDA: *(Gently humorous.)* Well, I think my grades would suffer.

BARB: I know this isn't the first time we've discussed this. But you keep bringing it up, Mom, and I can't seem to change your mind. *(Sighing.)* At this point, I just don't know what you want from me.

GERDA: I want your support, Barb. Not only to co-sign the loan. I value your opinion.

BARB: *(Shaking her head.)* I'm sorry, Mom. I just don't think this is a good idea.

GERDA: *(Firmly.)* I think it makes a lot of sense.

BARB: *(Defensively.)* I can certainly appreciate that you gave up your dream to raise your family. And that was a tremendous sacrifice. Don't think that that doesn't factor into my decision.

GERDA: Of course.

BARB: You were a great Mom. You ARE a great Mom.

GERDA: Well, thank you, Barb.

BARB: And of course I feel bad that I'm discouraging you from pursuing this. But you understand that I'm just looking out for what's best for you.

GERDA: Yes, I understand.

BARB: *(Sighing with relief.)* Well, good. I'm glad that's settled.

(GERDA does not respond but looks off to the side, thinking. Beat.)

BARB: Mom? What are you thinking?

GERDA: I was just thinking…maybe it would be cheaper to go to a state school instead.

END

The Grateful Dead

THEME: Jesus raises dead man.

SCRIPTURAL REFERENCE: "Then he went up and touched the coffin, and those carrying it stood still. He said, "Young man, I say to you, get up!" The dead man sat up and began to talk, and Jesus gave him back to his mother." *Luke 7:14-15.*

DRAMA SUMMARY: Man discusses his near-death experience and his second chance in life.

CHARACTERS:

LOU

DIANE

SETTING: A living room.

SCENE: LOU and DIANE are engaged. LOU is an open, enthusiastic man while DIANE is more cynical and wary. LOU wants to get married right away; DIANE has postponed the date several times. They sit on a couch together, facing the audience, as if they are watching television. A remote control lies on the coffee table.

DIANE: *(Gesturing to the television and protesting.)* Oh, please! That is *so* bogus!

LOU: *(Rationally.)* Now, Diane, there have been documented UFO sightings.

DIANE: *(Dubiously.)* Right. Aliens stealing their eggs, then fertilizing and breeding them? Come on!

LOU: *(Defensively.)* Well, it *could* happen. *(Beat.)* Leave yourself open to the possibility.

DIANE: *(Firmly.)* It's not possible.

LOU: *(Countering.)* Of course it's possible.

DIANE: *(Grabbing for the remote control and pointing it at the audience.)* I'm changing the channel.

LOU: Wait! I want to see how it ends.

(They watch in silence for a moment.)

DIANE: *(Gesturing to the television.)* So, what is she saying? That the person was dead when he was dumped from the spaceship but now he's alive again?

LOU: Basically. *(Explaining.)* See, that character and the alien became friends.

DIANE: So the alien gave him his life back?

LOU: *(Nodding.)* Yes.

(DIANE laughs.)

LOU: Why are you laughing? You see doctors shocking people back to life on television every day. Why is this any different?

DIANE: Well, that's because they're not really dead. *(Gesturing to the television.)* But that person has been cold for over 24 hours.

LOU: So?

DIANE: *(Scoffing.)* People just don't come back from the dead like that. Not once they're *really* dead.

LOU: *(Matter-of-factly.)* I did.

DIANE: *(Puzzled.)* What do you mean?

LOU: I had a near-death experience.

DIANE: *(Shocked.)* You never told me this.

LOU: *(Shrugging.)* It was a long time ago.

DIANE: So, what happened?

LOU: I had a snowmobile accident.

DIANE: You fell through the ice?

LOU: Yes. I went under and…well, I drowned. Or rather, I froze. *(He shrugs.)* It was one or the other.

DIANE: *(Disputing.)* You didn't really *die.*

LOU: Yes, I did. I was clinically dead. I saw my body lying there. I heard everything that was going on. I was dead when the ambulance arrived at the emergency room.

DIANE: But they brought you back.

LOU: *(Nodding.)* They put me on a heart bypass machine and transfused me. Eventually, my body started working again.

DIANE: I don't think you were really *dead*. Your brain was still alive, even though your body wasn't responding on its own. Your soul was still intact.

LOU: I believe that I was dead. I got a second chance. It was a miracle.

(Beat.)

DIANE: So what was it like? You know, being *dead*.

LOU: Quiet. It was very quiet. I could hear the air. And it was warm. I always imagined death would be very cold, but it was…balmy.

DIANE: Did you see a white light?

LOU: No. I just watched everyone, that's all.

DIANE: Were you afraid?

LOU: No. It felt very calm. I don't even remember thinking that I wanted to come back. I was comfortable being there.

(Beat.)

DIANE: What do you think it is that makes one person die and another person live?

LOU: I kind of wondered that myself. *(Beat.)* If I was clinically dead, why did I come back? Was it something so special about *me*, or did God have some unfinished business in my life? *(Beat, he shrugs.)* I don't know. I'm just here. And I'm grateful.

END

The King And I

THEME: Accountability.

SCRIPTURAL REFERENCE: "Do not be deceived. God cannot be mocked. A man reaps what he sows." *Galatians 6:7.*

DRAMA SUMMARY: Unhappy woman burdened by the inconvenience of the holiday season receives a visit from the Ghost of Christmas Future (in this case, Elvis).

CHARACTERS:

JENNY, Leslie's sister

LESLIE, Jenny's sister

ELVIS, in a sequined costume, wig and sideburns

VOICE

SETTING: Living Room.

AUTHOR'S NOTES: *The King and I* is my favorite drama. I love its visual possibilities and the *snap-out-of-it-ness* of its message. It was my friend Ann Marie, a brilliant actress/singer, who told me that we reap what we sow. In order to achieve personal happiness, she said, we have to make others happy. If we want to be loved, we have to plant the seeds of love first. ¶ *The King and I* is the most enjoyable script I've ever written and more than a little cathartic. I re-read it when I'm discouraged, and it's like a good kick in the pants to help me get back on track.

SCENE: *The set is JENNY's living room, decorated for Christmas. There are plates of cookies or candy dishes in various places. Several stockings are hanging to convey the presence of a family. There is a Nativity Set on a table. LESLIE enters. LESLIE is wearing a bulky winter coat and a visually-amusing winter hat, like a hunting cap with earflaps. She carries shopping bags and stomps grumpily as she walks. She kicks off her boots (or struggles to pull them off) when she arrives and drops her coat on the floor.*

LESLIE: *(Entering, dumping Christmas bags and packages on a table, irritated.)* Ugh! *(Calling.)* Jenny, I'm back.

JENNIFER: *(Entering, carrying her coat.)* Hey, Leslie. So, what did you think of the new Mall? *(She picks up LESLIE's coat and hangs it on the back of a chair.)*

LESLIE: *(Shrugging, unimpressed.)* Looks the same as the last time I was here. *(Grumbling.)* The crowds were a nightmare.

JENNIFER: *(Putting on her coat.)* I'm not surprised, since you hate shopping. *(Conversationally.)* Why are you so crabby?

LESLIE: *(Groaning.)* Christmas isn't the same as when we were kids. I mean, it used to be so much fun, but now it's just a big inconvenience to come back every year. *(Complaining.)* Nobody has any time to do anything. Nobody ever appreciates what I get them. *(Beat, thinking of another complaint.)* And I always go home sick. I don't even make plans for New Year's anymore because I always catch your kids' mutant germs at Christmas.

JENNIFER: *(Calmly, she is kidding.)* We do that on purpose. We feed them low doses of antibiotics to intentionally breed super bugs for you to catch when you visit. *(She puts on her hat.)* Listen, I need to run to the store. Will you be all right by yourself for awhile?

LESLIE: *(Waves her off with her hand.)* I'm fine. *(She pulls a small statue out of her bag.)* Hey, I bought you something. *(She holds it up for JEN-NIFER to see.)*

JENNIFER: *(Dismayed.)* Is that…an Elvis figurine?

LESLIE: *(Shrugging.)* I figured since I broke the shepherd in your nativity set, I'd replace it.

JENNIFER: *(Firmly, in a motherly warning tone.)* Don't put that thing in my stable, Leslie! *(She exits and turns back, shaking her finger, warningly.)* And don't re-arrange my furniture while I'm gone.

(JENNIFER exits. LESLIE waits until she's gone and then waves the statue in the air like a child with a toy airplane, playing with it, and zeroes in on the nativity set.)

LESLIE: *(Intoning.)* Jenny has *left* the building. And Elvis has arrived! *(She places the statue in the nativity set.)*

(The character of ELVIS enters and strikes an "Elvis" pose.)

ELVIS: Thank you. Thank you very much.

LESLIE: *(Turns and gasps.)* Who are you?

ELVIS: *(Pointing at the figure in her hand.)* Don't go putting me in with the shepherds, now. *(He points to himself.)* I'm the King.

LESLIE: *(She looks at the statue and explains.)* Oh, *that!* I was just trying to annoy my sister by putting this tacky statue in her nativity set. *(Hastily.)* No offense.

ELVIS: *(He helps himself to a cookie from the table and chews it.)* None taken, ma'am. Actually, I feel kinda sorry for you. You got as much Christmas spirit as a mayonnaise sandwich without the onion.

LESLIE: *(Groaning, slumping in a chair.)* I hate the holidays.

ELVIS: How come?

LESLIE: *(Complaining.)* All this rushing and buying and going and doing, and for what? Nobody ever stops to think about what *I* want or need. *(She turns to him abruptly.)* Why are you here, anyway?

ELVIS: *(Turning his face from side to side, as if the audience is the mirror and he is checking his hair.)* I'm the Ghost of Christmas Future. *(He turns, snaps his finger and points to her.)* Girl, we need to *talk*.

LESLIE: *(Snickering.)* The Ghost of Christmas Future? *(Indignantly.)* Wait a minute…You think I'm a "Scrooge"?

ELVIS: *(Shrugging.)* If the blue suede shoe fits…

LESLIE: *(Protesting)* But I'm a very generous person! Look! *(She pulls items out of her shopping bag.)* I just spent 50 dollars on my brother's fiancée, and I haven't even met her yet!

ELVIS: *(Matter-of-factly.)* All I'm saying is a little self-analysis never hurt nobody.

LESLIE: *(Annoyed, she stands up, crosses her arms, and taps her foot impatiently.)* Fine…Let's go. Show me what a bleak future I'm headed for. I'll realize how I've taken everyone for granted, and vow to change my ways. Then we'll all have a merry Christmas, blah, blah, blah. *(She looks expectantly at ELVIS, who is not moving and barks, snapping her fingers.)* Let's go, go, go!

ELVIS: *(Calmly sits down and gets settled, munching from a bowl of candy.)* I didn't bring an *audio visual* presentation, if that's what you're expectin'. *(Shrugging.)* Besides, you already know your future.

LESLIE: *(Defiantly.)* No, I don't. *(Demanding.)* So tell me: Will I be loved? Will I be happy?

ELVIS: *(Matter-of-factly.)* You reap what you sow, Leslie. The seeds you plant today are what you're gonna harvest tomorrow.

LESLIE: *(Irritated.)* Well, what does *that* mean?

ELVIS: *(Explaining.)* If you want to be loved, you better start lovin' people yourself. If you want to be happy, then plant some happiness. *That's* your future.

LESLIE: *(Snorting.)* Please! That's a little too simple, even for Elvis.

ELVIS: Don't be cruel, Leslie. *(Earnestly.)* See, life's a journey. You pick up your paintbrush, and you paint your own paradise. *(Shrugging.)* Don't blame nobody else for it.

LESLIE: *(Defensively.)* I'm not!

ELVIS: You're all shook up 'cause your family don't live up to your expectations. Well, boo hoo. Get a life, Leslie. Make your own future. That's all I'm sayin'.

(ELVIS exits as LESLIE turns her back on him and starts pulling items out of her shopping bag.)

LESLIE: *(Ranting.)* I went to three stores to find this scarf for my brother, who's going to hate it anyway. My sister, of course, is going to return this book the minute she opens it…*(She turns and sees that ELVIS is gone. She looks at her gifts and sighs, slowly replacing the items in the bag. She looks up as she hears the Voice.)*

VOICE: Elvis…has *left* the building.

END

Taking Care Of Bus(y)ness

THEME: Mary and Martha.

SCRIPTURAL REFERENCE: As Jesus and his disciples were on their way, he came to a village where a woman named Martha opened her home to him. She had a sister called Mary, who sat at the Lord's feet listening to what he said. But Martha was distracted by all the preparations that had to be made. She came to him and asked, "Lord, don't you care that my sister has left me to do the work by myself? Tell her to help me!" "Martha, Martha," the Lord answered, "you are worried and upset about many things, but only one thing is needed. Mary has chosen what is better, and it will not be taken away from her." *Luke 10:38–42.*

DRAMA SUMMARY: Martha accuses Mary of not taking on enough work at the office.

CHARACTERS:

MARY

MARTHA

AARON, an intern

SETTING: Mary's office.

SCENE: MARY is calm and rational. Even though MARY doesn't agree with or respect MARTHA's viewpoint, she remains professional and detached from MARTHA's emotional stance. MARTHA is a worker bee who toils diligently but conditionally; she is hurt by the lack of recognition she receives for her efforts. MARTHA has busy body movements and sharp edge to her voice.
MARY and AARON enter and sit at a table, laughing.

MARY: *(Shaking a piece of paper.)* You know, Aaron, this is fantastic!

AARON: I'm really not trying to be a brown-noser, Mary. Although I must say, I am so flattered that you asked me to evaluate your performance.

MARY: Well, one of my annual objectives is to oversee your professional development. And I really wanted your input on whether you felt our measurables were met.

AARON: All I can say is that my internship has been excellent. You've been a mentor in the truest sense of the word, and what I've learned from working with you…well, it's been invaluable to me.

MARY: *(Looking at the evaluation.)* I am so proud of you! Beyond the fact that you said very kind things, your feedback is fantastic! This is one of the most comprehensive evaluations I've ever received. It really demonstrates how strong your management potential is. *(Beat.)* I even like that you weren't afraid to put in some constructive criticism. It's very well-rounded, very well-done. You did a great job!

AARON: Well, thanks, Mary. *(He stands to exit.)*

MARY: *(Calling after him.)* Let's go to lunch next week and celebrate. You pick the place.

AARON: Sounds great! *(He exits and runs into MARTHA on his way out.)* Hey, Martha.

MARTHA: *(Nodding to him.)* Aaron. *(She enters and sits down, noticing the evaluation form MARY is beaming at.)* What's that?

MARY: It's an evaluation form that Aaron filled out for me. *(She shakes the paper.)* I am *so* proud of him! He did such a good job.

MARTHA: *He* evaluated *you?*

MARY: Yes! Well, I know I'm his boss, but don't you think he should judge my performance when it comes to his own professional development? *(Admiringly.)* He gave me some terrific feedback.

MARTHA: *(A little irritated.)* I just don't see how you ever get any work done.

MARY: *(Surprised.)* Excuse me?

MARTHA: *(Complaining/)* Every time I come down here, you're sitting there chatting with Aaron or one of the other interns.

MARY: It's not like we're goofing around. It's important for managers to take the time to develop their people. Training isn't something you do in your spare time; it's an ongoing process. It's essential.

MARTHA: When do you have time to work?

MARY: We met or exceeded every one of our objectives last year.

MARTHA: *(Complaining.)* All I know is that *my* people are taking on more and more, and yours don't seem to be picking up the slack.

MARY: *(Dubiously.)* Well, who wants the *slack?*

MARTHA: Somebody has to do it!

MARY: *(Shrugging.)* Outsource it.

MARTHA: *(Pointedly.)* I'm just questioning what your priorities are.

MARY: *(Confidently.)* My priorities are people first, work second.

MARTHA: *(Surprised.)* Don't you mean the other way around?

MARY: No. *(Shrugging.)* I don't want my team to take on every single task possible; that's just not a good use of our time. I would rather focus on the long-term benefits of developing my team. It's better for the employee, and over time, it's better for the company.

MARTHA: But you don't seem to care that all this work is falling on *me* and *my* team!

MARY: Nothing's falling on you, Martha. You take it because it's *there.* *(Beat.)* Maybe you should step back and look at the big picture.

MARTHA: Me?

MARY: *(Rationally.)* You seem awfully concerned about how many tasks you've absorbed. But I just have to wonder: How many of those tasks are essential? How many are applicable to your objectives? How do they fit into your strategic plan?

MARTHA: *(Defensively.)* I work as hard as I can for the company… something which not everyone else is doing! *That's* my strategic plan!

MARY: Well, my strategic plan is to work as *smart* as I can. Spending time on professional development gives me three new managers by next year.

MARTHA: You're not doing your full share. You've *got* to pick up more!

MARY: *{Sighing.)* Why is this so important to you, Martha?

MARTHA: *(Furiously.)* It's the principle! *(She huffs.)* I think we need to escalate this matter to a higher level.

MARY: *(Calmly agreeing.)* If you want.

MARTHA: *(Threatening.)* I'm not kidding, Mary!

MARY: Martha, I respect your skills and the fact that you work hard. But detach! Sit down and evaluate your priorities!

MARTHA: *(Not listening, scribbling in her planner.)* Let's set up a meeting for next Wednesday at three. I'll notify everybody.

MARY: *(Giving up.)* Whatever.

MARTHA: *(Grimly.)* I'll also book a conference room and send out a confirmation.

MARY: *(Humoring her.)* Fine.

MARTHA: *(She is still writing as she exits and turns back to Mary.)* Should I order beverages?

END

Advice With Dr. Flo

THEME: The Causes of Sin.

SCRIPTURAL REFERENCE: Jesus said to his disciples: "Things that cause people to sin are bound to come, but woe to that person through whom they come. It would be better for him to be thrown into the sea with a millstone tied around his neck than for him to cause one of these little ones to sin. So watch yourselves." *Luke 17:1-3.*

DRAMA SUMMARY: Radio psychologist Dr. Flo gives advice about getting along with people.

CHARACTERS:

DR. FLO, a radio advice columnist

HERMAN, GLORIA, PETER & BRENDA (voice-overs)

SETTING: A radio station.

AUTHOR'S NOTES: The questions posed to Dr. Flo are intended to mirror the situations described by Jesus in Luke 17.

SCENE: DR. FLO *is a middle-aged radio psychologist. DR. FLO is very confident that she knows what is best for her callers. She listens intently, then responds bluntly, but with love. Her trademark phrase, "Listen to me," is stated emphatically, while wagging her finger. Callers to the radio show are not visible to the audience.*

DR. FLO *enters, sits at a desk, and puts on a pair of headphones to resume broadcasting her radio show.*

DR. FLO: And we're back. If you just tuned in, this is Advice with Dr. Flo on KS32, the only call-in show with the guts to tell it like it is. Today we're talking about getting along with people. *(She presses a console button.)* This is Dr. Flo, you're on the air.

HERMAN: Dr. Flo?

DR. FLO: Yes, you're on the air.

HERMAN: *(Depressed.)* Oh, I don't even know where to start. Um, my name is Herman. *(Sadly.)* No one likes me.

DR. FLO: *(Politely.)* Why don't they like you, Herman?

HERMAN: Actually, the parents tell the kids in school to stay away from me.

DR. FLO: *(Concerned.)* Is this some kind of racial prejudice thing?

HERMAN: No, it's my job. I'm a salesman. Um, I sell pharmaceuticals at the schools.

DR. FLO: *(Nodding.)* I see, I see. *(Patronizingly.)* Gee, that really is too bad.

HERMAN: *(Mournfully.)* Because I'd like to be their friend, but they don't want to be around me. What should I do?

DR. FLO: *(Echoing.)* What should you *do*? You're a drug dealer, Herman. You're scum! *(Beat.)* Your answer is simple: Flush the stuff and become a productive human being!

HERMAN: *(Offended.)* Hey, I didn't call in to be judged—

DR. FLO: *(Interrupting.)* Listen to me! You're the worst of any creature alive because you're leading children to hell. Huh? What do you say to that, Mr. *Pharmaceutical Salesman*? *(She pushes a button and disconnects the call. She answers another call.)* Dr. Flo, you're on the air.

GLORIA: Hi, Dr. Flo. My name is Gloria.

DR. FLO: What's your story, Gloria?

GLORIA: *(Complaining.)* I'm having a really hard time getting along with a friend of mine. She's always saying things about me behind my back and trying to influence my friends. I've confronted her about it, but she keeps doing it.

DR. FLO: What is it that upsets you specifically?

GLORIA: *(Giving examples.)* She tells people lies about me. And she's always twisting my words around. She makes everything sound like I'm criticizing her, when I'm not.

DR. FLO: *(Matter-of-factly.)* She's a jerk.

GLORIA: *(Surprised.)* Well, yeah. *(Beat.)* So what should I do?

DR. FLO: *(Simply.)* Nothing. You already told her that this is bothersome, haven't you?

GLORIA: Yes. But she hasn't stopped.

DR. FLO: *(Bluntly.)* She's not going to stop. She's a jerk. Forgive her. She'll do it again. Forgive her again.

GLORIA: But—

DR. FLO: Face it, Gloria. Short of stuffing a dishtowel down her throat, you can't make her stop. The only behavior you control is your own. Learn from this: Make nice and watch what you say around this so-called *friend. (She disconnects her and connects to another call.)* Dr. Flo, you're on the air.

PETER: Hi, Dr. Flo, this is Peter.

DR. FLO: So why aren't you getting along with people, Peter?

PETER: *(Agitatedly.)* You won't believe this, Dr. Flo! I just took some friends of mine out to dinner last night, and they told me they didn't want to see me anymore.

DR. FLO: Why is that?

PETER: *(Disbelievingly.)* They keep accusing me of trying to buy their friendship! This is, like, the fifth time they've done this!

DR. FLO: Are you?

PETER: *(Admitting.)* Well, they're always talking about money and how tight things are. I guess I *do* pay a lot. I've tried to be discreet about it. *(Beat.)* But I really did think we were friends. What do I do?

DR. FLO: What do you mean "what do you do?" They told you already. You're toast. *(Beat.)* Learn to listen, and you wouldn't have gotten in the situation in the first place. *(She disconnects him and takes another call.)* Dr. Flo, you're on the air.

BRENDA: Hi, Dr. Flo, this is Brenda.

DR. FLO: Why don't you get along with people, Brenda?

BRENDA: You tell me. *(Whining.)* I'm a good person. I go to church. I volunteer. I spend time with my family. But everyone takes me for granted. *(Sniffling.)* Why don't people like me?

DR. FLO: *(Sympathetically.)* Brenda, it sounds like you're looking for some recognition.

BRENDA: *(Sniffling, thinking she is going to be praised.)* Yes, I guess I am.

DR. FLO: *(Sharply.)* Well, you're not going to get it here.

BRENDA: *(Confused.)* What?

DR. FLO: Look at you, sitting around and whining that no one likes you for doing the things that you're *supposed* to do! Listen to me! You don't get credit for not running stoplights! You don't earn kudos for feeding your children! You're not a better person because you didn't cheat at canasta! Did it ever occur to you that you're just a big cry-baby and *that's* why no one likes you?

(DR. FLO disconnects her.)

DR. FLO: *(Sweetly.)* And that's all the time we have here today. This is Dr. Flo on KS32, bidding you a gentle good afternoon.

END

What Goes Around, Comes Around

THEME: Humility.

SCRIPTURAL REFERENCE: "But many who are first will be last, and many who are last will be first." *Matthew 19:30.*

DRAMA SUMMARY: A college professor discovers a top student has plagiarized an essay.

CHARACTERS:

PROFESSOR MARTIN, a college Genetics Professor

JOSHUA, an average-grade college student

SETTING: A college classroom.

SCENE: *JOSHUA is an undergraduate student at the University. He is bright and articulate but is torn between pursuing a career as a bassist in a rock band versus pursuing a degree in genetics. His grades are good but not superior.*

The PROFESSOR is a man in his fifties who wears jeans and a tweed suit coat. He is easy-going but listens intently. He is a good judge of character and sees enormous potential in JOSHUA.

JOSHUA enters, sits at a desk, and begins grading papers. The PROFESSOR enters, carrying a briefcase.

PROFESSOR: *(Greeting him.)* Morning, Joshua.

JOSHUA: *(Greeting.)* Hey, Professor.

PROFESSOR: How's the grading going on my essays?

JOSHUA: I'm about halfway through. *(He hands him half of the stack.)*

PROFESSOR: *(Complimenting him.)* I can't tell you what a fantastic help you've been this semester.

JOSHUA: *(Admitting.)* It's a bit intimidating—working in this environment, that is.

PROFESSOR: Being surrounded by the eggheads in the Genetics Department, you mean?

JOSHUA: Well, yeah. You've got all these superstar post-doctorates on your roster, you know, and I'm just a "B" average undergrad. *(Beat.)* Are you sure I'm qualified to grade an essay on "The Role of Genetics in the 21st Century?"

PROFESSOR: *(Shrugging.)* So many of my students have turned into studying machines by the time they reach the graduate level. They sit in front of books and memorize facts and figures without any real comprehension of the implications or possibilities.

JOSHUA: *(Nodding, waving some papers.)* Like cloning animals simply for scientific achievement, without considering the ramifications it could have on human life.

PROFESSOR: Exactly! You, Joshua, have a wonderful ability to visualize and apply your knowledge to real life. *(He sits on the edge of the desk.)* I'm curious to hear your opinions.

JOSHUA: *(Flattered to be asked.)* I was disappointed that there was not much variation in either concept or analysis.

PROFESSOR: I'm not surprised. Go on.

JOSHUA: Almost everybody wrote about cloning. But there was no consideration given to the use of the application or what controls would be warranted in the next millennium. The essays only address how it could be accomplished. *(Beat.)* But there was one paper that was fantastic…*(He rummages through the papers to find it.)* Yeah, Ken Barker!

PROFESSOR: The Science fellowship winner?

JOSHUA: Now, I'm not saying this because the guy is absolutely brilliant, which everyone knows. But his paper totally blew me away! It was amazing!

PROFESSOR: What was the topic?

JOSHUA: He analyzed the genetic composition of incarcerated felons and then projected the probability of a new generation of highly aggressive individuals. He even factored in the impact of the death penalty to anticipate geographical deviations!

PROFESSOR: *(This topic is familiar to him.)* Really.

JOSHUA: He cited statistics on the likelihood of felons to have children with multiple partners and then found case studies which analyzed the long-term impact on the children and their probability of committing crime. Oh, it's phenomenal! You've got to read it! *(He hands him the paper.)*

PROFESSOR: I already have. *(He scans the paper briefly.)*

JOSHUA: *(Puzzled.)* What do you mean?

PROFESSOR: It was published last year. The *real* author is a former student of mine.

JOSHUA: *(Shocked.)* Oh, no. He plagiarized it? *(Beat.)* What should I do?

PROFESSOR: I'll take care of it. We have guidelines for this sort of thing. *(Beat.)* But a more interesting question for you to ponder now…Do you still find this environment intimidating, knowing that the greatness around you might not be all that meets the eye?

END

Automobile Repairs

THEME: Envy of evildoers.

SCRIPTURAL REFERENCE: "Do not fret because of evil men or be envious of those who do wrong; for like the grass they will soon wither, like green plants they will soon die away." *Psalm 37:1.*

DRAMA SUMMARY: Auto repair customers profit from unethical and illegal business schemes, while the honest patron is scorned.

CHARACTERS:

KENT, an inside-trader

GEORGIA, an insurance scam professional

WALLY, an honest Pinto owner

CLERK, auto repair shop manager

SETTING: An auto repair shop waiting room.

SCENE: The customers are sitting on a bench in an auto shop, waiting for their vehicles to be repaired. WALLY reads a newspaper.

KENT: *(Sipping coffee.)* Now this is what I call great service! Coffee, croissants, and repairs while you wait!

GEORGIA: *(Confiding.)* I wouldn't leave my car anywhere else.

KENT: *(Pointing.)* Yours must be the blue Beemer next to my Porsche.

GEORGIA: Yes. On the left of that purple...Pinto.

(KENT and GEORGIA both turn to look at WALLY, who slowly raises the newspaper in front of his face, sinking lower in his chair, embarrassed.)

KENT: I didn't think they made Pintos anymore.

GEORGIA: *(Confiding.)* I made a fortune off of a $250 Pinto. As soon as the recall notice went out, I found the first one I could get my hands on. That car blew up faster than you could say "insurance money."

WALLY: *(Listening, horrified.)* Your car exploded when you were driving it?

GEORGIA: No, no! *(Confiding.)* Staged the whole thing with a can of gasoline and a dimestore mannequin.

WALLY: *(Confused.)* But.. but...that's insurance fraud!

GEORGIA: *(Shrugging.)* Who's to say it couldn't have happened? The probability was at least 50/50.

WALLY: *(Sighing.)* No wonder my premiums are so high.

(The automobile shop CLERK enters.)

CLERK: *(Apologetically, to GEORGIA.)* Ms. Smith, your vehicle suffered structural damage this morning when you backed into your neighbor's garage. We feel responsible for this as an audit of our records reveals we did not specifically caution you about the need to check your rear-view mirror when driving in reverse. *(Sympathetically.)* You have our sincere apology on this hideously inappropriate lapse in service.

GEORGIA: *(Grimly.)* What are you prepared to offer me?

CLERK: *(Consolingly.)* Well, no amount of compensation can offset the insult of injury, but we will provide you with a loaner at no cost, and repair the damage for free.

GEORGIA: *(Grimly.)* And the neighbor's garage?

CLERK: *(Smiling.)* Consider it done.

GEORGIA: *(Nodding, satisfied.)* Yes, I think that's a suitable arrangement. *(She rises to exit.)*

CLERK: Here are the keys. *(Extending a tray of croissants.)* Croissant for the road?

GEORGIA: Why, thank you. (She *takes a croissant and departs, happily.)*

CLERK: *(Calling after her.)* Have a wonderful day! *(Beat, adding.)* Check your rear-view mirror when backing out!

(WALLY has been observing the exchange and approaches the CLERK.)

WALLY: *(Confused.)* I don't understand. Why would you pay for something that was so clearly her fault?

CLERK: *(Shrugging, unconcerned.)* Ms. Smith is one of our best customers. *(Confiding.)* Buys a new Mercedes Benz every year...*(pointedly)* and pays *cash. (He turns away.)*

WALLY: *(Sitting down, muttering to KENT.)* That's *so* unfair. It's always the users in the world who get a free ride. Is that injustice or what? *(Indignantly.)* Just once, I'd like to be the guy who drives through stoplights and cheats at golf. *(Sighing.)* Yeah, one of these days.

(KENT chuckles as he reads the newspaper.)

WALLY: *(To KENT.)* What's so funny?

KENT: *(Smiling.)* My stock dropped.

WALLY: *(Confused.)* Isn't that bad?

KENT: Well, ordinarily, but…*(He lowers his voice and confides in WALLY.)* This company is planning to merge with another company next month. With the stock dropping, I can buy twice as many shares now before the news becomes public and the price goes through the roof.

WALLY: *(Confused.)* But…but…that's insider trading. Isn't that illegal?

KENT: *(Winking.)* Not if I don't get caught.

WALLY: *(Musing, sadly.)* I received two shares of stock as a wedding gift. That's my entire investment portfolio.

KENT: *(Snickering.)* Gee, why not splurge and buy a third?

WALLY: I don't have that kind of money. *(Brightly.)* But, on the other hand, I sleep very well at night.

KENT: *(Shrugging.)* Me, I've been an insomniac since I sold the family business for scrap. *(Sighing.)* The stress is killing me. *(He puts his hand on his stomach, worriedly.)* I think I've got an ulcer. But who's got time to get it checked?

(The CLERK approaches.)

CLERK: Mr. Jones, your vehicle is ready.

KENT: Ahhh. How much do I owe?

CLERK: No charge, sir. *(Aside.)* Milt just wanted to say thanks for the stock tips and to let you know that any kind of service you need, it's on the house. *(He winks broadly.)*

KENT: Terrific! *(He tears a corner from the newspaper with stock information.)* Listen, give this to Milt. Tell him I'll be in touch. *(He stops abruptly, holds his stomach and groans, then exits.)*

WALLY: *(Standing, indignant.)* What kind of place is this, anyway?

CLERK: *(Startled.)* Sir?

WALLY: *(Scolding.)* What's going on here? Why are you rewarding people for illegal behavior?

CLERK: *(Not understanding.)* Oh, our standards for customer service are very high. `

WALLY: *(Disputing.)* You're *enabling* unethical conduct! *(Accusingly.)* You know who you remind me of?

CLERK: *(Hopefully.)* Someone famous?

WALLY: You remind me of the guy who used to lend his apartment to my brother-in-law, when he was cheating on my sister Molly. See, he made it so *easy* for him to be unfaithful that he might as well have been the cheater himself.

CLERK: *(Insulted, he changes the subject.)* I see. Now regarding the status of your vehicle…

WALLY: *(Impatiently.)* The purple Pinto.

CLERK: *(Icily.)* Yes. The carburetor needs a complete overhaul. *(Speaking carefully.)* It does not appear that we can service that particular…*make* during our regular hours. *(Artificially polite.)* Did you try the auto shop at the state prison? Perhaps they could fit you in.

WALLY: *(Wearily.)* But I've been waiting for over three hours. *(Sighing.)* I don't suppose it would still be under warranty?

CLERK: *(Starts to laugh, then composes himself.)* No. In fact, I doubt they even sell Pinto parts any more, to be honest.

WALLY: *(Hopefully.)* Free service for a good customer?

CLERK: Frankly, sir, but your car, *ahem*, is the type we prefer to…outsource elsewhere. *(Confidentially.)* Having it on site upsets the other customers. *(He pointedly shoos WALLY away.)* If you wouldn't mind exiting from the back door, that would be *wonderful. (He tosses him his car keys.)*

WALLY: Oh. *(He exits, shaking his head and talking to himself.)* I *do.* I *do* mind. *(He turns back to the CLERK and shouts in frustration, like a child.)* It's just not FAIR! *(He stamps his foot and stomps out.)*

END

Lost In The Translation

THEME: The Bible.

SCRIPTURAL REFERENCE: "Do not let this Book of the Law depart from your mouth; meditate on it day and night, so that you may be careful to do everything written in it. Then you will be prosperous and successful. Have I not commanded you? Be strong and courageous. Do not be terrified; do not be discouraged, for the Lord your God will be with you wherever you go." *Joshua 1:8-9.*

DRAMA SUMMARY: Scholars translate the Old Testament.

CHARACTERS:

RACHEL, the supervisor

JEREMY, the new employee

NAT, a scholar, a young boy

ANN, a scholar

DAVID, a scholar

SETTING: A translation house in 200 B.C.

AUTHOR'S NOTES: *Lost in the Translation* is a fun drama to introduce the Old Testament. The costumes are Biblical to illustrate the time period, but some references are intentionally modern to draw the audience into the story.

SCENE: NED, ANN and DAVID sit, writing painstakingly with quill pens on parchment. RACHEL and JEREMY enter. It is JEREMY's orientation at his new employment at a translator house. RACHEL carries a clipboard. All of the characters are in Biblical dress with sandals.

RACHEL: *(Concluding.)* And finally, Jeremy, this is the translator's room, where you'll be stationed. *(She grabs a large quill from a table and starts to write on the clipboard.)* What's today's date?

JEREMY: The 25th.

RACHEL: *(Scribbling as she repeats.)* October 25th, 200 B.C. *(She tears off a page and hands it to JEREMY.)* Here's your New Hire Authorization Form. Give it to Personnel when you leave today. *(Beat.)* Do you have any questions?

JEREMY: Well, I'm anxious to get started. *(He points to the other workers.)* What's everyone working on?

RACHEL: They're transcribing a book called the Old Testament. They started 80 years ago, and it's likely to go, oh, another 50 or 60 years. *(Beat.)* Most of us won't even be alive when it's done.

JEREMY: *(Impressed.)* It must be very important.

RACHEL: *(Agreeing.)* It's extremely sensitive material. *(She flips through the clipboard.)* In fact, we need you to sign a confidentiality agreement. You're not permitted to discuss the project with the media or your family.

JEREMY: *(Joking.)* I'll have to cancel the press conference then, Rachel.

RACHEL: *(Seriously.)* We're very serious, Jeremy. The book is about God and His dealings with His chosen people. Our competitors are circulating conflicting materials which also claim divine inspiration.

A council will be meeting soon to determine which writings were legitimately inspired by God...and which weren't. *(She scans the room, worried.)* The fate of the company is riding on this.

JEREMY: *(Signing the paper.)* So, who wrote the book? Anyone I know?

RACHEL: It's an anthology of books from many authors. Some of them were kings, some were poets and some were prophets. *(Beat.)* Each scholar is responsible for translating a different book.

JEREMY: Which book will I get?

RACHEL: *(Checking the clipboard.)* The book of Haggai. It's only two chapters. Once you pass your probationary period, you'll move up sequentially to the longer books.

JEREMY: *(Confidently.)* I'm sure I'll advance in no time. Which translator has the longest book?

RACHEL: *(Checking her clipboard.)* That would be Ann. *(She points.)* She has the Psalms—150 chapters.

JEREMY: Yikes! *(He shakes his hand painfully.)*

RACHEL: *(Hastily.)* Oh, no, she loves it.

ANN: *(Rapturously, as she writes.)* "My soul finds rest in God alone; my salvation comes from him. He alone is my rock and my salvation; he is my fortress, I will never be shaken."

RACHEL: *(To JEREMY.)* The Psalms are poetry. It's very beautiful and moving. *(She looks at DAVID.)* No, I'm more concerned about David. *(Worriedly.)* He has the book of Numbers.

DAVID: *(In a monotone.)* "From Reuben, Elizur son of Shedeur; from Simeon, Shelumiel son of Zurishaddai; from Judah, Nahshon son of Amminadab; from Issachar, Nethanel son of Zuar; from Zebulun, Eliab son of Helon..."

RACHEL: It's a little dry. *(Shrugging.)* We're rotating him into something else by the end of the week. *(She perks up.)* Maybe Job. *(Confiding.)* The book of Job always makes you feel grateful for what you have.

(NAT giggles. RACHEL hears but doesn't look at him.)

RACHEL: *(Rolling her eyes and sighing.)* Grow up, Nat.

JEREMY: *(Curiously.)* Who's that?

RACHEL: That's Nathaniel Asher. *(NAT giggles.)* He's translating the Song of Solomon. *(Confidentially.)* It's a bit, *ahem*, risqué. *(NAT giggles, like a young boy reading erotica for the first time. Note: NAT's laughter is out of embarrassment; it is not lecherous.)*

JEREMY: *(Perking up.)* Really?

RACHEL: *(Dryly.)* Don't worry. You'll get your turn.

JEREMY: *(Clearing his throat hastily.)* No, I just meant that I'm anxious to read all the books. It sounds like a fascinating compilation.

RACHEL: I've always dreamt of publishing a work that stood the test of time. Sure, we've had scrolls on the annual bestseller lists, but they fade from view as quickly as the seasons change. *(Wistfully.)* What wouldn't I give to publish a book that will endure through the ages…that's as timeless tomorrow as it was yesterday and today. *(Sighing, she turns back to JEREMY.)* Come on, Jeremy, I'll show you the lunchroom.

END

Life And Death

THEME: Regret, second chances.

SCRIPTURAL REFERENCE: "Godly sorrow brings repentance that leads to salvation and leaves no regret, but worldly sorrow brings death." *2 Corinthians 7:10.*

DRAMA SUMMARY: Teenage girls at a slumber party contemplate death, regret, and second chances.

CHARACTERS:

SUSIE, a teenage girl

CINDY, a teenage girl

HEATHER, a teenage girl

MARLA, a teenage girl

SETTING: Susie's home.

SCENE: *A slumber party for teenage girls. The set is a couch, chair and table. The girls are in pajamas, sitting on the floor, drinking soda from cans with bendy straws. One is initially lying backwards on the seat of the couch with her feet against the couch back and her head hanging over the side, facing the audience. There is an open pizza box and a bowl of pop-corn on the table. There are sleeping bags and pillows on the floor.*

HEATHER: Okay…*(She holds up two shoes.)* Black pumps or strappy sandals?

CINDY: *(With certainty.)* Pumps.

SUSIE: *(Disagreeing.)* Sandals!

MARLA: *(Offering her opinion to CINDY.)* I liked the boots you had on yesterday.

HEATHER: *(Changing the subject.)* Let's turn off the lights and tell scary stories!

CINDY: I don't want to…

SUSIE: Why not?

CINDY: *(Complaining,)* They give me nightmares.

MARLA: *(Suggesting.)* Well, how about scary stories about *true* things.

SUSIE: Oh! I have one! My Uncle Jack was driving drunk last year, and he crashed into a street sign. He lost his leg *and* his driver's license.

HEATHER: That's not scary; that's *sad. (To CINDY.)* What do you have nightmares about?

CINDY: *(Dramatically.)* Well, there's this tidal wave, and it washes over everything. And I feel myself pulled underwater, and I start to panic because I'm drowning.

MARLA: In my dream, I'm dancing at the prom, and I don't have any clothes on.

HEATHER: I always have a nightmare that I forgot to study for a test.

SUSIE: I had a dream once that my parents died. And it was awful because I had just had a fight with my Mom, and I never said I was sorry. *(Relieved.)* I was *so* glad when I woke up!

HEATHER: *(Beat, casually.)* So, which one of us do you think is going to die first?

CINDY: *(Protesting.)* Shut up, Heather! I don't want to talk about *that*!

HEATHER: *(Shrugging.)* Why not? Kids die all the time.

MARLA: *(Introspectively.)* I always think, what if I died, and people read my diary! I mean, I've written some *terrible* things about people. *(Beat.)* It's all true, but I never write any of the good stuff down.

HEATHER: *(Warning.)* You don't get another chance to take it back, you know. Once you're gone, that's it.

SUSIE: *(She holds a flashlight under her chin to create a shadow, like she's telling a ghost story.)* There was this boy who died when he was 12. And his parents were so busy all the time that they never paid any attention to him. But when he died, they completely freaked out, because they never made time for him when he was alive. And it's too late now.

CINDY: *(Agreeing.)* That *is* really scary.

HEATHER: *(Authoritatively.)* Okay, here's a question: What do you think people will say about you at your funeral?

CINDY: *(Proudly.)* My grandmother will say that I was a good role model for my sisters. She's always telling me that I have that responsibility as the oldest.

MARLA: People will probably make something up, just to make it look like they knew who I was. *(Beat.)* I'm sure they'll say nice things, but they won't be *true*. And that makes me sad, because that means they never really knew me in the first place.

SUSIE: I think my family will say how much they'll miss me.

HEATHER: *(Beat.)* Okay, here's a different question: If you knew you were going to die in 10 minutes, and you could only talk to one person, who would it be?

CINDY: *(Objecting.)* Heather! That's gross!

HEATHER: *(Ignoring CINDY, adding.)* And what would you say to that person?

MARLA: I'd call a family meeting...

CINDY: *(Protesting, pointing to HEATHER.)* She said *one* person!

MARLA: *(Stubbornly.)* Well, there's a lot to say!

SUSIE: Like what?

MARLA: I'd tell my grandfather that I thought he was generous with his money but that he was really stingy with his approval. My parents, on the other hand, I'd tell them how much I appreciated their staying up late every night, just talking to me. And I'd tell them that everything I am was because of them, and I'd thank them. *(She laughs.)* They'd die of shock! I *never* tell them stuff like that!

SUSIE: I'd tell my sister I was sorry for all the awful things I've done to her. Then if there was any time left, I would thank her for putting up with me. And I'd tell her that I would genuinely miss her and hope that she would miss me, too.

CINDY: *(Reluctantly.)* Well, if I knew I was going to die, I'd call up my friends and ask them to come over, so that we could be together right until it was time. Then I'd say goodbye and tell everyone I loved them.

HEATHER: *(Dramatically.)* I'd visit my Aunt Diana. She's this walking train wreck; her life is so out of control! I would tell her to get her act together because *her* time was right around the corner, too! Then I'd make her hold my hand and watch me die, to try to scare some sense into her. *(Beat, grimly.)* If that doesn't work, nothing will.

END

Simeon's Rap

THEME: Simeon at the temple.

SCRIPTURAL REFERENCE: "Now there was a man in Jerusalem called Simeon, who was righteous and devout. He was waiting for the consolation of Israel, and the Holy Spirit was upon him. It had been revealed to him by the Holy Spirit that he would not die before he had seen the Lord's Christ." *Luke 2:25-26.*

DRAMA SUMMARY: Simeon tells the story of meeting Jesus at the temple.

CHARACTERS:

NARRATOR

RAPPER

CHORUS (optional)

SETTING: In the temple.

AUTHOR'S NOTES: *Simeon's Rap* is one of my favorite dramas. What I particularly like is that the words remain constant, while each artist's interpretation is unique. It was commissioned by Acts 29, the High School Drama Ministry for Wooddale Church more than 10 years ago when rap music was still a novelty, but the concept of searching for God is timeless. Since then, I've seen five other productions of it. Two in particular stand out: My friend Jesse, a poet, performed it solo at Patrick's Cabaret, and the joy and simplicity in his performance literally left me in tears. My second favorite was a slow, haunting rendition by a group of visiting nuns at St. Peter's Church, accompanied on guitar, who transformed it into a Buddhist chant of sorts, overlapping the chorus with a reverent echo.

SCENE: The NARRATOR enters, holding a large Bible, and reads the Scripture aloud.

NARRATOR: "Now there was a man in Jerusalem called Simeon, who was righteous and devout. He was waiting for the consolation of Israel, and the Holy Spirit was upon him. It had been revealed to him by the Holy Spirit that he would not die before he had seen the Lord's Christ." *(He exits.)*

(The remainder of the drama is performed as a rap. Music and/or movement is defined by the artist.)

VERSE 1:

My name is Simeon; I'm the one

Been waiting my lifetime to see God's son

Today's the day, I heard the Spirit say

Go to the temple, to bow and pray

CHORUS

O holy God, amazing grace

I cannot die until I see your face

I long to feel your sweet embrace

I shall not die until I see your face

VERSE 2:

I'm a godly man of good repute

The Savior I have long pursued
My only vision, since my youth
Today the rumors became truth

CHORUS
Your soul inhabits this holy place
I cannot die until I see your face
My heart rejoices with a song of praise
I shall not die until I see your face

VERSE 3:
My life I've dedicated to the Lord
Through triumphs and trials my spirit's soared
For the glory of God is my reward
I'll worship His name forevermore

CHORUS
The wonder has set my heart ablaze
I cannot die until I see your face
My hands to you I humbly raise
I shall not die until I see your face

VERSE 4:
I cradled the child in my arms and cried
I wanted to speak but could only sigh
The walls echoed in reply

They knew the Savior should be glorified

CHORUS

You are the lamp that lights my way.
You are the sun at the break of day
You are the color beneath the gray
You are my source of joy today

At your feet I can only gaze
I will not die, I have seen your face
My spirit has listened and obeyed
I shall not die, I have seen your face

END

Author! Author!

THEME: The Bible.

SCRIPTURAL REFERENCE: Then the Lord said to Moses, "Write down these words, for in accordance with these words I have made a covenant with you and with Israel." *Exodus 34:27.*

DRAMA SUMMARY: A book reviewer, waiting to meet the author of a Bible study book, discusses the origins of the Bible.

CHARACTERS:

LAURA, a book reviewer

MARK

CUSTOMERS

SETTING: A book signing at a bookstore.

SCENE: LAURA *is a newspaper columnist. Previously a news reporter, she is used to pushing her way into a crowd with confidence to get a story.* MARK *is a man with a nice personality who often finds himself taken for granted in relationships. He is wary of women in general but is hopeful that he will meet someone with whom he'll be compatible.*

MARK *enters and stands in line in front of the table, waiting for the author.* LAURA *tries to sneak in front of* MARK. *She is holding a copy of a very large book.*

MARK: *(To LAURA.)* Excuse me! You're cutting!

LAURA: Sorry. *(Looking behind her.)* Look at this line! I'd really appreciate if you'd let me in.

MARK: *(Protesting.)* I've been here for hours.

LAURA: *(Holding out her hand to shake.)* I'm Laura Clark from the Daily *News.* I'm writing a review of Mr. Lamson's new book, and I just need to ask him a couple questions for my article.

MARK: *(Reluctantly.)* Well…

LAURA: Please…I've got a deadline.

MARK: *(Relenting.)* All right.

(They stand and wait, silently.)

LAURA: *(Enthusiastically.)* This is such an exciting book! I hear that several filmmakers are vying for the movie rights.

MARK: *(Agreeing.)* It's a great story.

LAURA: It's an epic! I mean, it covers 1600 years!

MARK: Originally written in Hebrew and Greek, too.

LAURA: That will really boost the foreign market.

MARK: Forty different authors contributed to the original work, you know.

LAURA: *(Puzzled.)* Original? Mr. Lamson didn't write it?

MARK: No.

LAURA: Well, what did he adapt it from?

MARK: That book *(he taps the book she is holding)* is completely based on the Bible.

LAURA: You're kidding! *(She flips through the book.)*

MARK: No. Don't you recognize the theme? The promise of salvation.

LAURA: *(Agreeing, but not really understanding.)* Oh, yeah. *(She begins scribbling notes, as she realizes that MARK's information is helpful.)*

MARK: *(He points to the book she is holding.)* The first half of this book is about law and morality. The second half is about redemption.

LAURA: *(Parroting what he says.)* You're right. That *is* taken from the Bible.

MARK: Small wonder! The Bible is the ultimate bestseller! It has everything—history, philosophy, poetry!

LAURA: *(Jokingly.)* Think they can cut it down to a two-hour movie?

MARK: Maybe a mini-series—a LONG mini-series. It's a progressive revelation from beginning to end.

LAURA: I see. *(Beat.)* Maybe a regular series then. *(Blurting.)* Who's the lead character, anyway?

MARK: Well, *God. (Suspiciously, to Laura.)* Have you ever read the Bible?

LAURA: Well, *parts. (Admitting.)* Actually, no. Not from start to finish.

MARK: *(Encouragingly.)* You should. It's an amazing story! In fact, you should read the *book* first, and then the books *about* the book!

LAURA: That's a good point.

MARK: *(Excitedly.)* You know, God is a real presence in our lives. He's the greatest story in history and the most exciting ongoing saga I can imagine.

LAURA: You've convinced me. *(Beat.)* So, why are you here, anyway? Are you going to buy the book?

MARK: *(Sheepishly pointing to the sign.)* He's my cousin. I wanted to say hi.

END

Half-Buried In The Snow

THEME: Spiritual renewal.

SCRIPTURAL REFERENCE: "Restore to me the joy of your salvation and grant me a willing spirit, to sustain me." *Psalm 51:12.*

DRAMA SUMMARY: Man dealing with relationship problems gets his car stuck in the snow on his way to work.

CHARACTERS:

BEN

STEVE, Ben's neighbor

SETTING: The driveway between the neighbors' homes on a cold day.

SCENE: BEN enters, with a shovel in hand. He is dressed in winter clothing, with big, heavy boots. He walks around, looking at an imaginary car offstage, as if he is trying to determine exactly where it is stuck in the snow. He leans on his shovel, pondering. STEVE enters and approaches BEN.

STEVE: *(Greeting.)* Hey, neighbor! Plowed in again?

BEN: *(Dismayed.)* I can't believe this! My tax dollars just paid the city to dump three feet of snow at the end of my driveway! *(He gestures at his driveway.)*

STEVE: *(Offering.)* Need a hand?

BEN: No, I got it. *(He continues to look at his driveway.)*

STEVE: *(Stands and looks offstage with BEN, philosophically.)* It's always important to deal with whatever's blocking your path.

BEN: *(Irritated.)* I know.

STEVE: But you have to be careful—sometimes the problem might not be what's on top, but what's underneath.

BEN: *(Reiterating.)* I *know.*

STEVE: In fact…

BEN: *(Venting at STEVE.)* For crying out loud! I get your point!

STEVE: *(Oblivious to STEVE's anger, walking toward the driveway and pointing.)* You're spinning on ice, Ben.

BEN: *(Sighing, looks at his watch.)* I'm going to try rocking it.

STEVE: *(Warning.)* That could spin your wheels deeper.

BEN: It depends on how stuck I am. *(He starts to walk offstage, then turns to lecture STEVE.)* Sometimes you just need to back up and try again a few times. *(He turns back to walk up the driveway and slips, landing flat on his back.)*

STEVE: *(Leaning over to address the prone BEN, calmly.)* Well, ice can be deceptive. It looks so safe, so you keep going and wham! *(He slaps his hand.)* You're flat on your back.

BEN: *(Still lying on his back, trying to maintain his dignity.)* I can see that.

STEVE: You just need something to hold on to, to get a grip on the ice. *(STEVE gives BEN a hand to sit up. They sit down on the ground together.)* You okay there, Ben?

BEN: I think I hurt my back. *(Beat.)* Marilyn and I are having some problems. We're talking about separating for a while.

STEVE: I'm sorry. *(Beat.)* You know, getting your car stuck in the snow is not unlike getting stuck in a relationship.

BEN: *(Not listening to STEVE, thinking aloud.)* But I just can't deal with it right now. First things first: I've got to get my car out. *(He stands, suddenly consumed with an idea.)* You know, sand would give me some good traction.

STEVE: *(Following BEN, still on the previous conversation.)* I mean, think about it. Your relationship is cruising along, everybody's happy, then suddenly there are patches of ice here and there that make your wheels spin, and you don't feel like you have quite as much traction anymore. There's always a warning—slow down, watch where you're going—but you ignore it, thinking it won't happen to you.

BEN: *(Not looking at STEVE, pointing to his imaginary car and groaning.)* Why didn't I put my chains on back in November? *(Beat.)* Why didn't I shovel *before* trying to get out?

STEVE: *(Continuing.)* Then the snow gets deeper and deeper. You're gunning your accelerator a little more, and the wheels are starting to spin. Before you know it, you've got a full fledged snowdrift up to your trunk!

BEN: *(Now listening to STEVE, but still only talking about cars.)* See, that's why you've got to invest the bucks in a good shovel. Too many people just drive their cars into three feet of snow and then act surprised when they…*(he looks at his car and sighs)* get stuck.

STEVE: If you heed the warning signals, you can deal with it *before* it becomes a barrier.

BEN: *(Giving up.)* I guess I went too far. *(Beat.)* What do I do now? How do I get unstuck?

STEVE: You've got to be able to recognize when you need help.

(BEN groans and waves STEVE off.)

STEVE: Believe me, I know. The hardest thing in my life was calling a plumber after I remodeled my bathroom. I had to learn to swallow my pride. I called for help.

BEN: *(Admitting.)* I guess you're right.

STEVE: *(Stands up and looks at the car.)* So, you need a hand?

BEN: With the car? *(Beat.)* Or my marriage?

STEVE: *(He looks at the car.)* Well, both, buddy. *(Determinedly.)* But let's get the car out first.

END

Control

THEME: Anger.

DRAMA SUMMARY: Unable to express his emotions, John channels everything into anger. He is angry with his wife, yet is afraid to communicate. When confronted by his sister-in-law, John explodes.

CHARACTERS:

EMOTIONS: ANXIETY, SELF-PITY, EGO, GUILT, ANGER

JOHN, main character

JACKIE, John's sister-in-law

SETTING: An empty stage with a ladder or wooden chairs.

AUTHOR'S NOTES: *Control* is about anger and how it can build as a response to other emotions during a seemingly innocent conversation. The script is based on a story told to me by my friend Patrice, whose brother-in-law was forced to commit his wife for treatment for alcoholism. ¶ *Control* is not a comfortable drama. It's intended to be unsettling and force the audience to feel the rage simmering within the character of John.

SCENE: The set is an empty stage with a large ladder or chairs of varying heights. In front is a bench on which JOHN and JACKIE will sit. The backdrop is black, and each of the characters is dressed in black. The tone is about shadows and mood.

JOHN enters, wearing a party hat and carrying a glass of punch, and he sits tensely on the bench. He is followed by each of the EMOTIONS (who are dressed like JOHN, wear party hats and hold punch glasses). The EMOTIONS stand behind and around the bench on the ladder or chairs, surrounding JOHN. ANGER stands at the top of the ladder or the highest position, directly above JOHN. He holds strings which are attached to JOHN's arms, jerking them as he is physically provoked by the voices of the other emotions. The EMOTIONS speak as if JOHN is thinking their thoughts. Their voices are exaggerated and grating.

The EMOTIONS speak their lines quickly, overlapping each other slightly. The character of JACKIE is cool and detached, which only fuels JOHN's anger. In this drama, JOHN becomes progressively angrier.

ANGER: *(Pointing at JOHN.)* Meet John Young, father of six. Two months ago, he committed his wife, Mindy, to a chemical dependency program. Today, he attends his first family function without her. *(Beat.)* John has been through the wringer lately. *(Gesturing to the other EMOTIONS.)* It's been hard on all of us, but particularly me. Frankly, I'm working overtime to carry these guys.

ANXIETY: *(Miserably.)* Rub our faces in it, why don't you? It's not like we don't have enough stress already.

ANGER: *(Angrily to ANXIETY, who shrinks in fear.)* Just shut up, will you? *(Beat, he introduces himself to the audience.)* I'm Anger. I'm the only emotion that John lets anyone see.

SELF PITY: *(Meekly introducing itself.)* I'm Self Pity. *(Beat, sadly.)* No one likes me.

GUILT: I'm Guilt. *(Beat, defensively.)* None of this would have happened if I hadn't interfered.

EGO: I'm Ego. *(Adding with self-importance.)* I don't *have* to share this ladder. I *choose* to share it.

ANXIETY: I'm Anxiety. *(Moans.)* I don't feel good. Is it warm in here?

(JACKIE enters and sits on the bench.)

JACKIE: *(Coolly.)* Hello, John.

JOHN: *(Calmly.)* Hello, Jackie. How are you?

GUILT: *(Panic-stricken.)* She thinks it's my fault that her sister drinks.

EGO: *(Pompously.)* I hope she's not planning to give *me* advice. After all, I'm not the one with the problem.

JACKIE: *(Politely.)* So, I heard that Mindy has been making progress since you last saw her.

ANXIETY: *(Agitated.)* What does she mean by *that*? I haven't seen Mindy since I left her in detox that night. She said she hated me.

GUILT: *(Wailing.)* She thinks I'm a terrible husband.

SELF PITY: *(Sadly.)* I *am* a terrible husband. I had terrible role models.

JOHN: *(Tensely.)* Glad to hear it. I just want to be as supportive as I can.

(JOHN and all of the EMOTIONS simultaneously raise their punch glass and drink in unison.)

JACKIE: *(Coolly.)* No one blames you for all this. *(Beat, irritated.)* But still, couldn't you have handled this in a less disruptive manner?

ANGER: *(Angry.)* Lay off!

EGO: This isn't about *me*! I don't make mistakes!

GUILT: *(Wailing.)* My children need their mother.

JOHN: *(Becoming angry.)* I tried everything. I tried to get her to talk. I took her to meetings. I even held an intervention. *(Defensively.)* It was the last resort. She couldn't take care of the children.

JACKIE: *(Neutrally.)* So, how are the kids coping without their mother?

ANXIETY: *(Hyperventilating.)* I don't want to be here. I feel sick to my stomach.

SELF PITY: *(Whining.)* Everything bad happens to me.

JOHN: They're fine.

ANGER & JOHN simultaneously: *(Snapping.)* They feel a lot better knowing their mother isn't going to die in a car crash tonight!

JACKIE: *(Calmly.)* Honestly, I don't see why you're getting so angry. I was just wondering if Mindy would be home for Kimmie's birthday. *(Beat, pointedly.)* She always has a party.

EGO: I've done everything I can do. Don't imply that I'm depriving my children!

SELF-PITY: Jackie is so ungrateful! She doesn't understand at all.

JOHN: *(Sharply.)* Mindy always took care of that.

JACKIE: *(Pointedly.)* Yes, but *Mindy* is locked away in a treatment center. Why don't *you* take care of it?

GUILT: *(Worriedly.)* It'll be my fault if she starts drinking again.

ANXIETY: *(Moaning.)* My heart is pounding. The room is getting smaller. I am having difficulty breathing…

JOHN: *(Defensively, hyperventilating slightly.)* Planning Kimmie's party was Mindy's job, and Mindy can be very controlling. *(Shaking his head, emphatically.)* I just don't want to be responsible for any setback in her progress.

JACKIE: *(Surprised.)* You can't plan your own daughter's birthday party?

SELF PITY: *(Meekly.)* I don't want to make her angry.

EGO: *(Indignantly.)* She has no right to be angry with *me*.

ANXIETY: I don't want to make her angry.

JOHN: *(Firmly, he is shaking with anger.)* I don't want to upset her. It'll make her angry.

JACKIE: So what if she's angry? Look how angry *you* are, just thinking about it.

(The EMOTIONS begin overlapping each other until the end.)

ANGER: *(Exploding.)* She can't talk to me like this!

EGO: *(Accusingly.)* Does she think I'm afraid? Because I'm not afraid.

ANXIETY: *(Pleading.)* Please don't let me cry. Not now. Please, not now.

GUILT: *(Sighing.)* I'm a terrible person. Something like this would never happen to a good person.

ANGER: *(Angrily.)* How dare she talk to me like this! I just want to spit in her face!

(JOHN and the EMOTIONS simultaneously remove their party hats. JOHN becomes more and more tense, until he is shaking with anger.)

EGO: I have better things to do than suffer another function with my wife's family!

ANXIETY: The walls are closing in on me! I need air!

GUILT: If only I loved her more, none of this would have happened. I didn't try hard enough.

ANGER: *(Angrily.)* I hate her! I hate her more than I've hated anyone in my entire life!

JACKIE: John, just calm down.

JOHN: *(Suddenly standing, shouting angrily.)* I'm NOT angry!

(Beat. The EMOTIONS are startled into utter silence.)

JACKIE: You're furious. *(Beat.)* Why do you let it control you like this? *(She exits. JOHN sits on the bench for a moment, then also exits.)*

END

At What Cost, Survival?

THEME: Expendability.

SCRIPTURAL REFERENCE: The eye cannot say to the hand, "I don't need you!" And the head cannot say to the feet, "I don't need you!" On the contrary, those parts of the body that seem to be weaker are indispensable, and the parts that we think are less honorable we treat with special honor. *1 Corinthians 12:21–23.*

DRAMA SUMMARY: Parody of the Reality Show "Survivor" with a new twist: the Christian family.

CHARACTERS:

JEFF, the television show host

JOHN & SUSAN, the Miller Family father and mother

BEN, John and Susan's son

SARAH, the babysitter

SETTING: On the set of the *Survivor* television show.

SCENE: JEFF enters, followed by the four family members, wearing hiking clothes and carrying torches. JEFF addresses the congregation as if he is speaking into a television camera.

JEFF: *(To the audience.)* Good evening, everyone. I'm Jeff Parker, host of "Survivor Family" on WCRS, Christian TV.

(Dramatically.) We're minutes before the Tribal Council vote on our 31st day. For viewers just tuning in, we secluded eight members of the Miller clan at their family cabin, waiting for their Christian veneers to crack under the pressure of 24x7 scrutiny and the chance to betray their familial bonds.

Each week the remaining family members have voted another one out, and we are now down to the Final Four. When just two players are left, the family will form a jury to decide the winner of a one million dollar prize and the title of *Christian Survivor!*

Let's meet the Final Four: John and Susie Miller, their son Ben, and—the surprise underdog—the babysitter.

SARAH: *(Shrugging.)* No surprise there, Jeff. The Millers respect me more than their own family members. In fact, the more I charge, the better they treat me. *(She laughs.)* Go figure.

JEFF: Let's review the previous episodes: The first contest was a physical challenge which took its toll on John's mother, Nana. *(A photo of NANA displays overhead.)* Survivors, let's talk about your strategy and why you decided Nana was the first to go.

BEN: Nana slowed us down. We cut her loose.

JEFF: *(Surprised.)* Just like that? No remorse?

SUSAN: It was a strategic decision, Jeff. *(Adding.)* Frankly, Nana's such a giving person, it was easy to take what we needed. *(Beat.)* She was expendable.

JOHN: *(Adding.)* It hurt Mom's feelings, of course, but she'll get over it.

(JEFF is shocked and open-mouthed, turning back and forth between JOHN and the audience, speechless.)

JEFF: The next Castaway was Uncle Mike, John's brother. *(A photo of MIKE displays on the screen.)* Ironically, we learned that Mike rescued his brother in a swimming accident when they were children. John, any regrets about voting off the man who literally saved your life?

JOHN: *(Decisively.)* No. It wasn't personal.

JEFF: Well, if it wasn't personal, why persuade the others to vote off Mike?

JOHN: *(Explaining.)* Mike was the strongest physically and represented the biggest challenge to me as the leader. *(Adding.)* I'm not beholden to anybody. I'm here to win.

JEFF: *(To the audience.)* The most shocking vote occurred in episode number three when this Christian couple formed an alliance to vote off their daughter, Polly. *(A photo of POLLY displays on the screen.)* Your thoughts on this heart-wrenching decision, Susan?

SUSAN: *(Slowly.)* Voting off your own child is unthinkable, Jeff. *(Sighing.)* I hadn't anticipated casting out my kids for at least another week. *(Defiantly, to the audience.)* But Polly was just too devoted to God. *(Firmly.)* There was no way we could have withstood a threat like that in the Final Four. *(Adding.)* She made the rest of us look bad.

JEFF: *(Puzzled.)* But isn't the whole point of the game, Susan, to be the Christian who survives life's challenges with his faith and integrity intact? Someone who makes decisions based on God's will for his life?

SUSAN: *(Snorting.)* That lasted about a day, Jeff. Our focus now is on the money.

JEFF: *(Discouraged, he turns to the audience.)* On a sad note, one of the kindest players I've ever encountered—Melvin, the Miller's Next-Door Neighbor—was voted off in episode four. Your thoughts, John? *(A photo of MELVIN displays on the screen.)*

JOHN: *(Waving him off dismissively.)* I knew from Day One that I could exploit Melvin's faith. Christians are givers, Jeff. I'd be a fool not to use that to my own advantage.

JEFF: *(Sadly.)* That brings us up to the last two weeks. Now, the babysitter—

SARAH: *(Popping up, cheerfully.)* Sarah!

JEFF: *(Continuing.)*—Sarah—won both of the Family Memory challenges, which has kept her in the game. What was your strategy, Sarah?

SARAH: *(Explaining.)* Well, I'm the expert on the Miller family. *(Adding.)* They tell me all their secrets.

JEFF: *(To SARAH.)* Winning the contests gave you immunity from the last two votes. With only immediate family left, do you think you're vulnerable today?

SARAH: Not at all. *(Confiding.)* Mr. Miller doesn't know that Mrs. Miller and I have formed an alliance to vote him off next.

JEFF: *(Turning to BEN.)* Ben, you're still in the game, too, buddy. What do you attribute that to?

BEN: Everyone knows my Mom's in charge. She and I have an alliance to the Final Two.

JEFF: But your Mom apparently has alliances with all of the remaining survivors, Ben. How do you know she won't betray you, like she did your sister Polly?

BEN: *(Confidently.)* I'm her oldest son. She'll either betray my Dad or sacrifice herself for me. *(Shrugging.)* Textbook psychology, Jeff. Either way, I'll win.

JEFF: *(To the audience.)* So there you have it: The Final Four in the Family Survival contest, heading to the Tribal Council vote now. *(He looks at the four and turns back to the audience, sadly.)* May the most deserving soul win.

END

The Cover Story

THEME: Christmas

DRAMA SUMMARY: Newspaper reporter is upset with her assignment: covering the news of Christ's birth.

CHARACTERS:

GEORGE, reporter

ANNA, frustrated reporter

JACOB, newspaper editor

MARK & ANDREW, reporters

SETTING: Newspaper office in Bethlehem, the day after JESUS' birth. A sign displays *Bethlehem Star & Tribune.*

SCENE: The characters are dressed in Biblical attire. GEORGE works at a manual typewriter. (Note: the typewriter, notepads and pens are intentionally not consistent with the time period.) ANNA enters and sighs noticeably, hovering.

ANNA: *(Innocently baiting him.)* So, what story are you working on, George?

GEORGE: *(Not looking up at her.)* Go away, Anna. You know very well what I'm working on.

ANNA: *(Annoyed.)* It's not fair! You get all the good assignments!

GEORGE: *(Holding up his hands defensively.)* Don't tell me. Talk to the Chief.

ANNA: *(Complaining.)* I'm tired of being the only woman reporter around here. And I'm tired of getting all the soft features. *(She bangs her hand on the desk, startling GEORGE.)* I want to do hard news, George! Just once, I want the cover story!

(JACOB enters briskly, followed by a group of reporters, notebooks in hands, taking notes furiously on their assignments.)

JACOB: *(Pointing.)* Andrew! You're doing the governor's speech.

ANDREW: Got it, Chief! *(He snaps his notebook shut and runs out.)*

JACOB: Mark!

MARK: Yes, sir?

JACOB: Go with Andrew. Get to the guts of what's cranking underneath. I want the dirt and the politics.

MARK: The underlying motivation?

JACOB: Exactly! *(Suspiciously.)* It's the first census by Quirinius. I want to know what role the governor is playing, and what his opponents are plotting now.

MARK: I'm on it, sir! *(He races out.)*

JACOB: George!

GEORGE: *(Snaps to attention, dashes to his side.)* Chief!

JACOB: *(He grips GEORGE's arm.)* I smell a big story here, George. I want to know how much money this census is costing the taxpayers. Thousands of people are flooding into Bethlehem. I want to know where the money's coming from and who's getting the kickbacks.

ANNA: *(Interrupting eagerly.)* I can take it, Chief!

JACOB: *(Hemming.)* I don't think you're ready yet, Anna.

ANNA: *(Protesting.)* I am! Look: *(She paints a picture for him.)* Bethlehem is overloaded. The streets are crowded. The inns are sold out. Not enough food. It's got all the angles, Chief—misery, poverty and the human condition!

JACOB: *(Narrowing his eyes, thinking.)* I like it.

ANNA: *(Modestly.)* Thanks, Chief.

JACOB: *(Turns to GEORGE, snapping his fingers.)* George! Get on it!

ANNA: Wait! It was my idea!

JACOB: *(Paternally.)* Don't worry, Anna-Banana…I've got something better for you.

ANNA: *(Excitedly, pleading.)* Let me interview Caesar Augustus then! I'll get him to crack! I know I can!

JACOB: *(Not listening.)* That's good, sweetheart. But here's what I want you to cover.

(ANNA stands poised, ready to take notes.)

JACOB: Everyone's in town for the census—all the hotels are booked.

ANNA: *(Nodding.)* Mm hmm.

JACOB: There's this great human interest story…

(ANNA groans and stamps her foot.)

JACOB: Pregnant lady couldn't get a room, so she had her baby in a barn.

ANNA: *(Protesting.)* Oh, come on!

JACOB: *(Encouragingly.)* Run with it!

ANNA: *(Protesting.)* It's so stupid! It's right up there with the donkey that could bray in perfect pitch.

JACOB: *(Shrugging.)* It's human interest. People like happy endings.

ANNA: *(Defiantly.)* I'm not doing it. I'm tired of holding out my cup and finding the last drop went to the person before me.

JACOB: *(Reasonably.)* Fine, pass it up. But remember, a good reporter can find an angle in any story.

(JACOB exits.)

ANNA: *(Glaring at GEORGE, snapping.)* Oh, go work on your story, George.

GEORGE: Sorry, Anna. *(Beat.)* So, what are you going to do?

ANNA: *(Determined.)* I'm going to interview Caesar Augustus.

GEORGE: But…but what about the pregnant lady?

ANNA: *(Sighing.)* It'll happen again tomorrow and the next day and the next day. *(She picks up her coat and exits.)* Believe me, nobody'll miss it.

END

Full Disclosure

THEME: Truth.

SCRIPTURAL REFERENCE: "A truthful witness gives honest testimony, but a false witness tells lies." *Proverbs 12:17.*

DRAMA SUMMARY: A seller tries to disclose a house's problems to an unsure homebuyer, whose brother is intent on a sale.

CHARACTERS:

RUTH, who is selling her home

JOHN, a first-time homebuyer, a little naïve

CARL, John's brother

SETTING: An Open House.

SCENE: CARL and JOHN enter together, then stand, waiting for RUTH to re-appear.

CARL: *(Enthusiastically.)* Isn't this fabulous, John? You're on the verge of buying your first home!

JOHN: *(Worriedly.)* Well, let's see whether I like it first.

CARL: You are going to *love* this place; I guarantee it! But no matter what, you can stay with Mom and me as long as you need. *(He pats him on the shoulder insincerely.)* Sure, space is tight, but that's what family is for. *(He pauses and looks at John.)* You're sure you don't want to find an apartment? *(Too hopefully.)* You could move out today.

JOHN: No, now that I'm back in town, Carl, I want a house of my own. *(He looks at a brochure.)* See? I've even got a list of questions: "How old is the furnace." "Copper plumbing." Stuff like that. *(Sighing.)* I just wish I knew more about this kind of thing.

CARL: *(Reassuring him.)* Trust me. I know exactly what to ask. *(Rubbing his hands happily.)* We'll get you out of my house in no time at all! *(Nudging JOHN as RUTH approaches.)* Here comes the owner.

RUTH: *(Apologetically.)* Sorry for that interruption.

JOHN: *(Politely.)* No problem.

RUTH: *(Continuing.)* As I was saying before, I'm dropping the asking price by $5,000 because of the window repairs.

JOHN: *(Worriedly, to CARL.)* Well, that's not a good sign if she's dropping the price, is it? Something must be horribly wrong.

CARL: *(A little too enthusiastically.)* It's great! That price is a steal for this neighborhood! And you can't ask for a better location! Close to restaurants, almost in the country, but right by a highway! *(To JOHN.)* Your commute to work will be 10 minutes, tops!

RUTH: *(Continuing.)* It's a lovely home but it does need some work. *(Adding.)* That's why I'm selling. I'm afraid I haven't been able to keep up with the maintenance. And the storms last summer only aggravated the problems.

CARL: *(Rationalizing to JOHN.)* All houses need a little tweak here and there to bring them up to code. Perfectly standard.

RUTH: *(Continuing.)* There's some water damage in the living room. And I'm afraid that there might be a problem with the roof.

JOHN: *(Doubtfully, to CARL.)* Maybe we should just go home.

CARL: *(Correcting JOHN's reference to "home")* You mean, *my* house.

JOHN: Yeah. *(Puzzled.)* What did I say?

CARL: *(Shaking off the scare.)* It's not so bad. *(Gesturing.)* Big deal, a couple of shingles fell off. The day you sign that mortgage, Mom and I will get up there and personally nail them back on for you.

RUTH: *(Disagreeing, stubbornly.)* The roof is fairly old. It really should be replaced.

JOHN: *(Worriedly.)* Well, is that expensive?

RUTH: *(Nodding sympathetically.)* It can be, yes. And it's very difficult to find a good roofer who's available these days.

CARL: *(Aside to JOHN.)* John...John...She doesn't know what she's talking about. *(He snickers.)* She can't even keep up with the basic maintenance.

RUTH: *(Handing JOHN a 14-inch paper document.)* Now, I had the house inspected, and here's a copy of the appraisal report. The problems that I mentioned were noted as exceptions, as you can see. *(She points out the items on the report.)*

CARL: *(Interrupting RUTH and snatching away the inspection report.)* You know what? Let's not worry about this now, John. Go check out that basketball court in back. *(He pushes JOHN to the exit.)*

JOHN: *(To RUTH.)* My brother knows how much I love to shoot hoops. *(He exits.)*

CARL: *(Waits until JOHN is out of earshot, then turns to RUTH, angrily.)* What's wrong with you, lady?

RUTH: *(Surprised.)* Excuse me?

CARL: *(Gesturing with his fingers.)* He's *this* close to buying, and you're scaring him off! Stop telling him what's wrong with the house! He's never going to move out!

RUTH: *(Stubbornly.)* Your brother needs to weigh *all* of the costs and the benefits equally. I *have* to be honest.

CARL: Tell him there's another buyer. Tell him they want to pay cash.

RUTH: I'm not going to lie just to sell my house to the first taker. This is a *commitment*. He needs to know that going in. *(She exits.)*

(JOHN walks back in.)

CARL: *(Pulling out a purchase contract.)* Isn't it a great house, John? Isn't it exactly what you're looking for?

JOHN: *(Agreeing half-heartedly.)* I guess I do like it.

CARL: *(Urging him.)* I think we should make an offer today. *(Lying.)* Look, I didn't want to say anything, but there's another couple interested, and they're willing to pay *cash*. You need to get something on the table, pronto.

JOHN: *(Worriedly.)* But what about the repairs? Shouldn't we find out more…

CARL: *(Interrupting.)* Standard pre-contract disclosure mumbo jumbo. Nothing for you to worry about.

JOHN: *(Worriedly.)* Well...Are you sure?

CARL: *(Nodding vigorously.)* Oh, yeah. *(Beat; he pulls out a purchase contract and starts to fill it out.)* So, what price should we start the bidding at?

END

Enemies

THEME: Loving your enemies.

SCRIPTURAL REFERENCE: You have heard that it was said, "Love your neighbor and hate your enemy." But I tell you: "Love your enemies and pray for those who persecute you, that you may be sons of your Father in heaven." *Matthew 5:43-45.*

DRAMA SUMMARY: Woman's mother is upset to learn that her daughter has been corresponding with her biological father.

CHARACTERS:

JOANNE, Kelly's mother

KELLY, about 30

SETTING: Kelly's home.

SCENE: KELLY and her MOTHER enter. They kneel on the floor, picking out baby clothes for a baptism.

KELLY: So, what do you think, Mom? Should Jenny wear the white gown or the pink dress for her baptism?

JOANNE: Definitely the white.

KELLY: *(Agreeing.)* And she can wear the dress for the party afterwards.

JOANNE: Did you get RSVP's from everyone?

KELLY: *(Shaking her head.)* Same as always. Everyone will just show up, and I won't have enough food.

JOANNE: I can throw together a salad, if you like.

KELLY: That might be a good idea. There could be a few extra people. *(Beat.)* I'd like to invite someone, Mom, but I wanted to check with you first.

JOANNE: It's *your* daughter's baptism. You don't need to check with me.

KELLY: *(Beat.)* I'd like Dad to be there.

JOANNE: Of course your father will be there. Didn't I tell you that his trip was canceled?

KELLY: Not Myron. *(Beat.)* My father.

JOANNE: *(Firmly, trying to cut off this conversation.)* Myron *is* your father.

KELLY: *(Intimidated, she hesitates.)* Well, yes, legally, Myron is my father. But I'm talking about John.

JOANNE: *(Sharply, cutting the conversation short.)* I don't want to hear another word about this.

(Long beat.)

KELLY: I know it's painful for you, but it's been 25 years since he left. Can't you forgive and forget?

JOANNE: *(Sharply.)* I said I don't want to discuss it.

KELLY: He says he's changed. He wants to be a part of my life now.

JOANNE: *(Shocked.)* You *talked* to him?

KELLY: *(Stammering.)* Well, he called. We've been in touch.

JOANNE: *(Sputtering.)* You went behind my back? Do you know how much pain this man has caused me?

KELLY: I didn't know if I wanted to talk to him either, at first. But I felt I owed him that. *(Beat.)* I want Jenny to know all of her grandfathers.

JOANNE: *(Angrily.)* I hate this man! I despise him more than you will ever despise anything in your life. *(Turning to KELLY.)* And to know that you're *talking* to him, that you're letting him into our lives again…

KELLY: *(Giving up.)* Look, just forget I said anything. Obviously, this was not a good idea. *(Beat.)* I'm sorry. I didn't mean to upset you, Mom.

JOANNE: Of course you upset me. *(Beat, bitterly.)* I can't believe you'd take the side of my enemy!

KELLY: I'm not taking sides. *(Beat.)* Like I said, it wasn't an easy conversation. I certainly had to swallow my pride. *(Beat.)* I hadn't realized how inadequate I've felt. It's pretty humiliating to have someone just walk away like that.

JOANNE: *(Bitterly.)* You barely remember it. *I'm* the one who had to deal with the aftermath!

KELLY: *(Mollifying her.)* You're right.

JOANNE: *(Dramatically.)* Honestly, you might as well just stab me in the back.

KELLY: *(Wearily.)* Mom, come on. My talking to John has nothing to do with you.

JOANNE: It has *everything* to do with me. What kind of a man leaves his wife with two small children?

KELLY: *(Explaining.)* He was at a different place in his life then. He feels terrible about it.

JOANNE: He's a drunk.

KELLY: *(Countering.)* He says he's been sober for two years. He's really trying to put his life back together and make amends.

JOANNE: *(Firmly.)* Well, not on my time, he's not. Not with *my* family!

KELLY: Mom, I'm sorry that my decision to see him is causing you pain. But I just can't turn down the opportunity to get to know him. I hope this doesn't come between us. *(Beat.)* Even if you can't forgive him, can you at least forgive *me*?

END

How Should I Greet Thee?

THEME: Mother's Day.

SCRIPTURAL REFERENCE: "Honor your father and your mother, as the Lord your God has commanded you, so that you may live long and that it may go well with you in the land the Lord your God is giving you." *Deuteronomy 5:16.*

DRAMA SUMMARY: Siblings shop for a Mother's Day card.

CHARACTERS:

GREETING CARD STORE CLERK

LINDA, Andy's sister

ANDY, Linda's brother

SETTING: A greeting card store.

SCENE: LINDA and ANDY are siblings. They enter, perusing a greeting card store, looking for a Mother's Day card for their mother. They hold several greeting cards in their hands, reading them. LINDA and ANDY approach each other.

LINDA: Did you find one?

ANDY: *(Gesturing with the card.)* Not really. There were some cards that were, you know, *okay,* but nothing that really jumped out at me.

LINDA: *(Sighing.)* Me, neither.

(The CLERK enters.)

CLERK: *(Politely.)* Is there anything I can help you with today?

LINDA: *(Gesturing with the cards.)* Oh, we're just looking for a card for our mother.

CLERK: *(Politely.)* We have a nice selection of Mother's Day cards over here. *(She gestures.)*

ANDY: *(Dismissing the suggestion.)* I've already gone through those. *(Sighing.)* Nothing.

CLERK: What exactly are you looking for?

ANDY: *(Suggesting.)* Well, she likes poetry. Something that rhymes.

LINDA: *(Adding.)* And she enjoys gardening. Maybe a flowery design?

CLERK: Like this? *(She points to one of the cards LINDA is holding.)*

LINDA: *(Firmly.)* Yes, but it's not right. It doesn't quite express how we feel about our mother.

CLERK: *(Politely.)* What would you like it to say?

ANDY: It needs to acknowledge how unselfish she is. I mean, it goes without saying that she gave up so much when we were kids, but even now, she's just always there for us.

LINDA: *(Chiming in.)* She's supportive and unbiased and always looks out for our best interests.

CLERK: *(Matter-of-factly.)* Sounds like a nice lady.

ANDY: *(Agreeing.)* She is. *(Adding.)* But she's no pushover. One of the things I like most about my mother is that she knows where she stands. She doesn't change just because someone else doesn't agree.

LINDA: That's so true. I can certainly list the many, many things that my mother has done or given me—

ANDY: *(Counting them off.)*—the school events, the family trips, the birthday parties—

LINDA:—but it's not about the tangible activities. It's not about what she *does*. It's about who she *is* inside.

CLERK: I know what you mean. A mother is someone special.

ANDY: *(Admiringly.)* She's the most gracious, generous, loving, talented, efficient, self-affirming, beautiful woman in the world.

LINDA: Don't forget "funny." *(Laughing.)* She has a great sense of humor.

ANDY: *(Agreeing.)* Oh, our mother is crazy. *(Clarifying, hastily.)* But in a good way.

LINDA: And compassionate. *(Beat.)* We were the only family on the block where the kids didn't want any more pets. *(Shaking her head in wonder.)* My mother is a magnet for lost souls.

ANDY: *(Warningly.)* But she can be tough. *(Shaking his head, chuckling.)* You don't want to meet her in a dark alley if you haven't picked up your lawn clippings.

CLERK: *(Carefully.)* That's a tough one to find in a greeting card.

LINDA: *(Sighing.)* I grew up thinking that my mother was perfectly ordinary and nondescript. It's only now—as a mother myself—that I've realized how extraordinarily gifted and precious she is. *(Sadly.)* She's just too rare.

CLERK: *(Doubtfully.)* That's a lovely sentiment, but I'll be honest with you. We don't have anything in stock that says all that. *(Beat.)* I'm sorry.

ANDY: We understand. Anyway, thanks for your time.

(LINDA and ANDY hand the cards back to the CLERK and begin to exit.)

LINDA: *(Complaining.)* This is the fourth store we've been to today. *(Sarcastic.)* What do they think we're going to do…tell her in *person?*

ANDY: I just don't understand. *(Beat, puzzled.)* What, don't greeting card writers have mothers?

(They exit.)

END

Only In My Backyard

THEME: Missions.

SCRIPTURAL REFERENCE: "And now, O Israel, what does the Lord your God ask of you but to fear the Lord your God, to walk in all his ways, to love him, to serve the Lord your God with all your heart and with all your soul, and to observe the Lord's commands and decrees that I am giving you today for your own good?" *Deuteronomy 10:12-13.*

DRAMA SUMMARY: Dinner guests deplore world suffering but decline to become involved.

CHARACTERS:

JOHN, the host

CAROLINE, the hostess

VICKI, a guest

LEONARD, a guest

GWEN, a guest

SETTING: A dinner party in a living room.

AUTHOR'S NOTES: The original version of *Only in My Backyard* was written for my friend Ian as a means of educating his sponsors when raising funds for his missions efforts. Since then, this drama has been requested the most and from the oddest places imaginable. This puzzles me because the script is not creative or clever or profound. Nevertheless, someone sees it and tells someone, then someone else sees it and tells someone, and so on, and so on, which is kind of cool when you think about it because that's really what missions is all about.

SCENE: *A couple invites friends over for dinner. The GROUP enters the living room, carrying cups of coffee.*

CAROLINE: Why don't we have our coffee in the living room? *(They sit.)*

VICKI: Wonderful dinner, John!

JOHN: Thanks, Vicki.

LEONARD: I don't think I've ever eaten homemade pasta before! It was delicious!

CAROLINE: Isn't it great? I gave John that pasta maker last Christmas.

JOHN: The machine is fantastic, except...

VICKI: What?

JOHN: *(Doubtfully.)* Well, it was made by Perrysberg.

LEONARD: So?

CAROLINE: *(Explaining.)* John feels that it's morally wrong to subsidize any company which contracts with overseas sweatshops.

VICKI: Awfully high standard to uphold, John. How do you even know?

JOHN: I get a watchdog publication. I also monitor companies who contribute to government funding in oppressed nations.

CAROLINE: *(Confiding.)* We sold all our stock in companies which outsource work to sweatshops.

LEONARD: But where do you draw the line, John? I mean, everywhere in the world, there are problems.

VICKI: Civil rights atrocities...

CAROLINE: Destruction of the rain forest for commercial development...

LEONARD: People killing each other in the name of religion...

VICKI: I read about suicide bombers driving through crowded market-places, armies killing civilians at random, and it sends a chill down my spine. Maybe it's cultural, but I just can't comprehend how this kind of thing can just happen every day.

CAROLINE: Not only that, but there's still so much oppression. People are being deprived of their right to express their beliefs freely all over the world.

LEONARD: At least in America, we still have the right to free speech. In another country, if I wanted to worship, say, a pumpkin, I could be thrown in jail for that.

(GWEN enters the room, listening.)

JOHN: *(Dismissively.)* Really, we're so much better off in the United States than anywhere else.

GWEN: In that case, I know you'll want to help sponsor my cousin's missions trip to Asia next spring.

(Silence.)

GWEN: You will, won't you?

VICKI: *(Cautiously.)* It's not the money, Gwen. You know we always contribute to a worthy cause.

CAROLINE: *(To JOHN.)* In fact, put me down for that food shelf fundraiser next week.

GWEN: But?

JOHN: *(Flatly.)* I don't invest money in countries that don't believe in God.

GWEN: *(Calmly.)* But doesn't that defeat the purpose of missions, John?

JOHN: *(Defensively.)* I boycotted lettuce for migrant workers' rights. I stopped buying Colombian coffee because of the drug trade. I'm not supporting efforts—humanitarian or otherwise—for countries that don't recognize basic civil rights.

CAROLINE: And why should we provide financial support for an effort that will at best gain an inch when that same support could gain a mile elsewhere? It's the *principle* of the thing.

GWEN: Don't you see? Those inches will multiply and divide and multiply again! Missions work can't be done in a day—but every inch is critical to gain a yard.

LEONARD: *(Grumbling.)* I don't think we should even be sending people overseas. It's dangerous, and frankly, no one invited them.

CAROLINE: Don't get me wrong, Gwen. It's certainly a noble cause. But I say let the sponsoring country support the missionaries. *(Reasoning.)* Every corporation has a chargeback process. God is no exception.

VICKI: If your cousin was working with the kids at the youth center or cleaning up the highway, I'd be the first to show you my checkbook. *(Emphatically.)* But I want to see the results here, and I want to see the results now.

JOHN: What results? A couple people say they believe in Jesus and then what, hmm? People are still killing each other. *(Beat.)* What I want to know is exactly what have they accomplished?

(NOTE: This drama is intended to be followed by a speaker, describing what missions work has accomplished recently.)

END

It Could Have Been Worse

THEME: Inconvenience.

SCRIPTURAL REFERENCE: "Consider it pure joy, my brothers, whenever you face trials of many kinds, because you know that the testing of your faith develops perseverance." *James 1:2.*

DRAMA SUMMARY: Three stranded travelers are rescued during a snowstorm and brought to a school shelter.

CHARACTERS:

LINDA

MARCIA, 50-ish

DAN

NATIONAL GUARDSMAN

SETTING: A school gymnasium.

SCENE: *The GUARD enters, followed by LINDA. They wear bulky winter coats, hats and boots. The GUARD wears a uniform and carries a flashlight. LINDA wears a dressy outfit under her coat.*

GUARD: *(To LINDA.)* We've set up the grade school here as a temporary shelter for travelers like you caught in the storm, ma'am. We've got cots set up in the gymnasium, and there are some sandwiches and coffee on that table over there. It's not the Ritz, but at least you'll be warm and dry.

LINDA: *(Fuming.)* I can't believe this! I should have been in Duluth two hours ago. Why can't you just pull my car out of the ditch?

GUARD: *(Politely.)* Even if we had the manpower to tow your car, we'd just be picking you up again two miles down the road. Nobody's getting through tonight. They're expecting 22 inches, plus drifting.

LINDA: *(Irritated.)* Am I supposed to be grateful? I'm missing the most important night of my life, and you act like I should pat you on the back and say, "good job." *(She takes off her jacket. She is dressed up.)*

GUARD: *(Noticing LINDA's outfit.)* Looks like you were headed somewhere fancy.

LINDA: I'm supposed to be on a stage right now receiving an award for my work with the homeless. And you can't even pull my car out of a ditch. *(Fuming.)* A two-year old could do it!

(MARCIA enters, somewhat in shock.)

GUARD: *(Suggesting.)* Why not think of how much you'll gain from this experience? Now you'll know how it feels to be homeless for a night, sleeping in a shelter with strangers. Maybe it will give you some insight into your charity work.

LINDA: *(Snapping.) Do not* patronize me. This is the *worst* night of my entire life!

GUARD: *(Countering politely.)* It could have been worse. Believe me, you are one of the lucky ones. *(To Marcia.)* Hello. Are you all right, ma'am?

MARCIA: *(To a person offstage)* Thank you again. It was very nice meeting you! *(Teeth chattering, to the GUARD.)* Thank God someone found me so quickly! I was afraid I'd freeze to death, but I was even more afraid of the silence! It's so deadly quiet out there. All those abandoned cars! I should have listened to my daughter and stayed home.

GUARD: *(Politely.)* Would you like some coffee to warm up? *(He pours coffee.)*

MARCIA: Oh, that would be wonderful! *(Confiding.)* You know, I just hate traveling in the winter. *(Looking around.)* But isn't this lovely? It's like a slumber party almost.

(DAN enters, with his hand wrapped in a paper towel.)

MARCIA: *(Worriedly.)* That man over there…I think he's hurt.

GUARD: Need some help, sir? *(He rushes over to DAN.)*

DAN: It's just a superficial cut. *(Worriedly.)* Of course, those bleed the most.

GUARD: Let me look at that. *(He examines DAN's cut.)*

DAN: *(Modestly.)* It's nothing, really. You know, I was mugged once while it was raining, and I suffered some broken ribs. It was very painful. *(Adding.)* But it's my personal motto never to complain.

MARCIA: *(Encouragingly.)* I think that's a very good attitude. My mother told me to always look on the bright side of life. No matter how bad things get, there is always a lesson to be learned.

LINDA: *(Sips coffee and spits it out in the cup.)* Ugh! This is the *worst* coffee I've ever tasted in my life! Is this instant? Is it too much to ask for *real* coffee?

DAN: *(Ignoring LINDA.)* My personal suffering has enriched my inner soul. After my appendix ruptured this fall, I made a vow to rechannel that pain back into a positive, healing medium.

LINDA: *(Fuming.)* Of all nights for this to happen. We haven't had snow for weeks!

DAN: *(Continuing.)* And I vowed never to let on about the chronic sinus irritation from my allergy medication. After my last visit to the emergency room for epinephrine after I got stung by a bee this summer, I said, "Dan, no one needs to know you have a bloody nose every morning."

MARCIA: *(Turning back and forth between LINDA and DAN, frowning.)* Oh, my.

DAN: Do you have any aspirin? I've got this horrible, pounding headache. It's right between my eyes. *(Beat.)* It's making me nauseous. *(Beat.)* I hope I don't throw up. The last time I vomited was…*(He pulls out a pocket calendar and flips through it.)* March 15th, 1995.

GUARD: Let me find that aspirin. *(He opens a first aid kit and hands DAN an aspirin.)* Here you go, sir.

LINDA: *(Demanding.)* Where is my car? Are you going to pull it out or not?

GUARD: The Desk Sergeant can give you a status report on your vehicle. I can take you to him, if you'd like.

LINDA: *(Exasperated.)* What have I been saying for the last half hour? *(To the others, threateningly.)* If there's as much as a scratch on it…

MARCIA: *(Laughingly, to LINDA.)* I don't care about my car! I'm just thankful to be *alive*!

DAN: *(Shrugging.)* I don't know. *(Pondering.)* Do I want to continue the ongoing struggle between good health and misery? Is life worth it? *(He shrugs.)* Overall, I'd say yes, but it's a fine line sometimes.

GUARD: *(To MARCIA.)* I think your attitude is commendable, ma'am. I hope your vehicle didn't suffer too much damage.

MARCIA: *(Defiantly happy.)* I hope it did! I never liked it anyway. Now I can get a red one with a sunroof!

DAN: *(Complaining.)* My car has been in the shop thirteen times in four months. After the brakes failed last December, they swore they inspected everything from top to bottom. But of course, that was before the fire…

(They walk out, exiting.)

LINDA: *(To DAN, irritated.)* Will you just shut up? *(Beat.)* You're really getting on my nerves.

END

A Time To Heal

THEME: Healing in God's time.

SCRIPTURAL REFERENCE: "There is a time for everything, and a season for every activity under heaven: A time to be born and a time to die, a time to plant and a time to uproot, a time to kill and a time to heal, a time to tear down and a time to build." *Ecclesiastes 3:1-3.*

DRAMA SUMMARY: Two strangers meet in a hospital waiting room and reveal their attitudes on healing.

CHARACTERS:

KRISTIN

MICHAEL

NURSE

SETTING: A hospital waiting room.

SCENE: *MICHAEL is being discharged after his last chemotherapy treatment. He is dressed in a T-shirt and sweatpants and wears a cap on his head. He moves slowly and painfully, although when sitting, it should not be overly-apparent to KRISTIN that he's ill.*
KRISTIN is dressed in a business suit and always carries work with her. She is a brisk woman, not terribly observant or tactful, and generally considers herself to be smarter and better than others.
The NURSE wheels MICHAEL into the waiting room and helps him into a chair. He carries a journal/book with him. He bends forward and puts his head between his knees for a moment. The NURSE sits in the chair next to him, puts her hand on his back, and waits for him to recover.

NURSE: Take a deep breath, Michael. *(MICHAEL inhales a few times.)* Better?

MICHAEL: Yes, thanks. I'll just sit here until my ride comes…try and catch my breath.

NURSE: *(Making conversation.)* So, that was your last treatment. You must be glad.

MICHAEL: Yes.

NURSE: *(Lightly.)* I'll miss seeing you around here.

MICHAEL: Me, too. *(Trying to thank her but still fighting for breath.)* You've been very kind.

NURSE: *(Picking up the book.)* What are you reading?

MICHAEL: *(His nausea subsides.)* Oh, actually I'm trying to get my affairs in order. You know, picking out the casket, the pallbearers…That sort of thing.

NURSE: *(Kindly, but not overly-emotional. She knows he's going to die.)* I'm sorry.

MICHAEL: *(Reassuring her.)* No, really, it's all right. In fact, it's very liberating. I'm making my peace with it. *(He breathes deeply.)* I'm feeling better. I'm okay now.

NURSE: Sure? *(He nods. She pats his hand and stands.)* I'm right around the corner if you need me. *(She exits.)*

(MICHAEL sits and reads for a moment. KRISTIN enters and sits down rapidly, spreading her papers out noisily. She looks around and shudders visibly.)

MICHAEL: *(Noticing her.)* Are you all right?

KRISTIN: *(Explaining.)* Ugh, I just hate hospitals.

MICHAEL: This place isn't so bad. At least it doesn't have that hospital smell.

(NURSE re-enters, looking for KRISTIN.)

NURSE: Kristin?

KRISTIN: Yes? *(She rises and approaches the nurse.)*

NURSE: Cathy is being moved out of the Recovery Room, and she'll be back in her room soon. If you want to go up, I'll take you there in a minute. *(She hands MICHAEL a pill and a cup.)* For your stomach, Michael.

(MICHAEL gestures his thanks and swallows the pill. KRISTIN sits and starts gathering her things.)

MICHAEL: Everything okay?

KRISTIN: Oh, yeah. *(She gestures offstage.)* My friend had a tonsillectomy this morning. They just took her to the Recovery Room.

MICHAEL: That's good.

KRISTIN: *(Shaking her head, stuffing papers in her briefcase.)* No, it's really a shame.

MICHAEL: What is?

KRISTIN: Her lack of faith! *(Turning to MICHAEL.)* Do you believe in God?

MICHAEL: Yes, I do.

KRISTIN: Do you believe He can heal people?

MICHAEL: *(Thinking.)* Yes.

KRISTIN: Well, obviously my friend didn't, or else I wouldn't be here right now.

MICHAEL: *(Disagreeing.)* I disagree.

KRISTIN: *(Challenging him.)* You said you believed that God heals people.

MICHAEL: For a purpose, yes. Nobody tells God what to do. If He intends to heal someone, they'll be healed. It's not measured by how much they believe. It's God's decision.

KRISTIN: *(Bitterly.)* She wasn't even willing to refuse the surgery. She just accepted it passively.

MICHAEL: I wouldn't presume to comment on that. Those kinds of choices really are private matters between the individual and God.

KRISTIN: *(Snapping.)* That's a cop-out! God expects us to take the risk!

MICHAEL: *(Ludicrously.)* What? How would *you* know?

KRISTIN: Because God healed me! I had a suspicious lab result, and I prayed about it. I had *faith!* When they re-tested, it was fine!

MICHAEL: *(Blankly.)* Well, a clean lab report is always good news.

KRISTIN: I never doubted that God would heal me. *(Heatedly.)* It just ticks me off to see people who are sick. Frankly, they're just getting their due.

MICHAEL: *(Embarrassed for her.)* I can't believe you're actually saying these things out loud. And you're not even embarrassed.

KRISTIN: *(Stubbornly.)* God can heal them!

MICHAEL: There's a danger in getting too caught up in praying for a specific outcome. *(Suggesting.)* Why not pray for yourself, for example, for wisdom in knowing what to do to help your friend?

KRISTIN: *(Stubbornly.)* Everyone needs to be healed. No one should be left behind.

MICHAEL: But you're saying that the ratio of faith equals the measure of healing. That's just not so. *(Beat, for emphasis.)* We're not *God*.

KRISTIN: *(Firmly.)* God said, "ask and you shall be healed." If they're not, it's because they didn't believe. *(She turns to Michael and puts her hand on his arm.)* God can heal you, too.

MICHAEL: *(Sharply.)* Look, you don't know anything about me. *(He is angry and wants to shock her.)* I'm dying, okay? I'm moving to a hospice and I'm getting ready to *die. (Kristin is shocked speechless.)* And, on top of *that*, now you're telling me that it's *my* fault! Do you think that's what I need to hear right now? Do you? Because maybe I need to make my peace. Maybe I need closure. Maybe what I need to hear is that I won't have to go through this alone. *(Beat, bitterly.)* You should *think* before you talk. You have *no idea* where I am in my life right now.

(NURSE enters.)

NURSE: I can take you up to Cathy's room now, Kristin. *(KRISTIN hastily gathers her papers, wanting to make a fast exit, embarrassed. MICHAEL regrets having snapped at her and tries to be kind.)*

MICHAEL: I hope your friend has an easy recovery. *(Beat.)* It's always harder for an adult to recover from a tonsillectomy.

KRISTIN: *(Beat.)* Thanks. *(She begins to exit then stops, not looking at MICHAEL.)* I'm sorry. *(She exits.)*

END

That Kind of Money

THEME: Greed.

SCRIPTURAL REFERENCE: Jesus replied, "Man, who appointed me a judge or an arbiter between you?" Then he said to them, "Watch out! Be on your guard against all kinds of greed; a man's life does not consist in the abundance of his possessions." *Luke 12:14-15*.

DRAMA SUMMARY: Distant relatives vie for a deceased man's fortune.

CHARACTERS:

LARRY, a probate attorney

MICKEY, a cousin

ARTHUR, a nephew

ELLEN, a niece

DONNA, a niece

SETTING: An attorney's office, with an urn and coffee cups on the table and a flip-chart on the wall.

SCENE: MICKEY, ARTHUR and ELLEN sit at a conference table in LARRY'S office. LARRY enters, holding papers.

LARRY: Good morning. Sorry to keep you waiting. I'm Larry Schaffer, Mr. Bennett's attorney.

MICKEY: *(Proudly.)* I'm Mickey Bennett. I'm a fourth cousin, twice removed.

ARTHUR: *(Eagerly.)* I'm Arthur Bennett. I'm the stepson of Mr. Bennett's third cousin's wife.

ELLEN: *(Snobbishly.)* Ellen DeBerg. I'm Mr. Bennett's fifth cousin, once removed.

LARRY: I'm very happy that you were all available to meet regarding Mr. Bennett's probate. As you know, he died intestate.

MICKEY: *(Puzzled.)* What does that mean?

LARRY: *(Explaining.)* Intestate means that he did not have a Last Will and Testament. Disposition defaults back to the laws of the state.

ARTHUR: So, you're saying that George's estate will probably be split among his relatives?

LARRY: Yes, if you're all in agreement. *(He looks around, and they shrug and nod their heads. He stands.)* Will you excuse me for a moment? I'll be right back. *(He exits.)*

ELLEN: *(Disparagingly.)* From what I know about George's side of the family, he probably had 50 bucks in a box under the bed.

MICKEY: *(Shrugging.)* I can't say I even remember George. What did he do?

ARTHUR: *(Vaguely.)* Some blue-collar thing. *(Beat.)* Or was he a technical writer?

ELLEN: *(Musing.)* Sad that he passed away though. Was there a funeral?

ARTHUR: *(Shaking his head.)* No one found him for days. The city finally cremated him. *(He gestures to the urn on the table.)*

MICKEY: *(Commenting.)* Oh. He died alone.

(They sit silently, unperturbed. Each character is occupied with him or herself. ELLEN applies lipstick. Arthur straightens his tie. Mickey cracks his neck and knuckles. LARRY returns.)

LARRY: All right, so it doesn't sound like we're looking at any legal disputes over the disposition of Mr. Bennett's assets.

ELLEN: *(Irritated.)* What are we talking about here? *(She looks at the others.)* Because if there are debts involved, I really don't feel I should have to pay anything.

MICKEY: *(Agreeing.)* That's a good point. *(He turns to LARRY.)* What are our legal obligations? I mean, at best, we're George's distant relatives. *(He looks to the others for confirmation, and they nod quickly in agreement.)*

LARRY: *(Correcting him.)* First, his name was *Gerry*, not George. And second, it does appear that the decedent's assets will cover any outstanding debts.

ELLEN: *(Exhaling.)* That's a relief. *(Suddenly interested.)* What kind of assets are we talking about?

LARRY: I don't have a complete accounting of his funds, so I can't give exact totals.

ARTHUR: *(Impatiently, snapping his fingers.)* Ballpark, Larry.

LARRY: *(Shrugging.)* Well, give or take a million…

(ELLEN starts to choke on her coffee.)

LARRY: *(Continuing.)* I'd put it in the range of $10 million, but a small part of that is tied up in investments.

MICKEY: Where did George—ahem, *Gerry*—get that kind of money?

ELLEN: *(Speaking carefully.)* I think we've established that I'm the closest living relative…

MICKEY: *(Interrupting her.)* No, you're not! I am!

ARTHUR: *(Interrupting.)* I disagree…It might help if we could map this out…*(He turns to LARRY and gestures to the flipchart.)* May I?

LARRY: By all means.

(ARTHUR begins furiously diagramming a family tree on the flipchart, tearing off pages and sticking them up on the walls and the podium.)

ELLEN: *(To MICKEY.)* Well, what if I took care of the liquid assets, and you two can split the investments.

MICKEY: *(Arguing to ELLEN.)* Didn't he just say that the investments make up only a small part of the 10 million?

ARTHUR: *(Diagramming.)* Now, a fifth cousin, once removed, and a fourth cousin, twice removed…

(They all speak at once.)

ELLEN: *(Heatedly, to LARRY.)* I was Gerry's favorite! He told me if anything ever happened to him, he wanted me to…

MICKEY: *(To LARRY.)* That money is mine! Nobody else is entitled to anything!

(The sound of a door knock. They all stop talking and look at DONNA, who enters.)

DONNA: Sorry I'm late. I'm Donna Bennett. *(They look at her blankly.)* Gerry's niece.

ELLEN: His *niece?*

(ARTHUR puts down the pen.)

DONNA: Yes, my father was Gerry's brother. I've been out of the country. I came as soon as I heard.

LARRY: Well, this just gets more and more interesting. *(To DONNA.)* There's been some uncertainty as to your uncle's final wishes.

DONNA: Not to worry. *(She hands a piece of paper to LARRY.)* I have notarized instructions from Uncle Gerry with specific bequests. He's allocated his entire estate among several research foundations. He also left specific instructions regarding a memorial service, and I'd like to arrange that. *(She looks at ELLEN, MICKEY and ARTHUR.)* It would be wonderful to have as many family members there as possible.

ELLEN: Of course. *(Standing up abruptly, looking at her watch.)* Look at the time. *(She exits.)*

MICKEY: *(To DONNA; he is lying.)* Absolutely! Just let me know when and where. *(To ELLEN.)* I'll walk out with you. *(He exits.)*

ARTHUR: *(Running after them.)* Want to split a cab to the airport? *(He exits.)*

DONNA: *(Sighing.)* Poor Uncle Gerry. He'll never know how much we miss him. *(LARRY pats her on the shoulder.)*

END

The Missions Statement

THEME: Missions, evangelism.

DRAMA SUMMARY: Interviewer surveys parishioners on the church missions statement.

CHARACTERS:

INTERVIEW VOICE

PERSONS 1-3

SETTING: On the street.

SCENE: *PERSON 1 walks across the stage and pretends to be stopped by the Interview VOICE. (Note: insert the applicable Church Name in the blanks below.)*

VOICE: Excuse me, do you have a minute?

PERSON 1: *(Looking around, trying to locate the source of the voice, puzzled.)* Uh, yeah, sure.

VOICE: I'm interviewing people at _____ Church and wonder if I can ask you a question.

PERSON 1: Well, what would you like to know?

VOICE: I'm surveying people to see how many know what _____'s Missions Statement is.

PERSON 1: *(Shakes his head.)* Sorry. *(Keeps walking offstage.)*

(PERSON 2 walks onstage, from the opposite direction.)

VOICE: Hi, do you know what a Missions Statement is?

PERSON 2: *(Surprised by the voice, but takes it in stride.)* Sure, I do.

VOICE: Do you know what _____ Church's Missions Statement is?

PERSON 2: *(Shrugging.)* I probably could paraphrase it.

VOICE: Go ahead.

PERSON 2: *(In an official business tone of voice.)* "_____ Church's mission is to effectively facilitate intercultural community relations via development, integration and cross-denominational communication so as to achieve an efficient capacity model and segregational parity."

(Beat.)

PERSON 2: *(Asking.)* Something like that?

VOICE: *(Beat.)* To be honest, I'm not even sure.

PERSON 2: *(Cheerily.)* Have a good day now! *(PERSON 2 waves and walks off as PERSON 3 enters.)*

VOICE: Good morning.

PERSON 3: *(Does a double take and looks upward.)* Hi.

VOICE: I'm taking a survey on the Missions Statement of _____ Church.

PERSON 3: Do you mean a Corporate mission statement, or do you mean a statement about the missions and outreach opportunities?

VOICE: Oh! I meant a statement about missions and outreach.

PERSON 3: They're two different things, you know.

VOICE: So, do you know what _____ Church's Missions Statement is?

PERSON 3: Well, Jesus said to go forth and make all men disciples. So, I assume it has something to do with that.

VOICE: That's pretty good.

PERSON 3: *(Keeps talking.)* And not just associating with people who are already disciples. We have to reach people where they are, not necessarily where *we* are.

VOICE: So would you quit your job and become a full-time missionary?

PERSON 3: Actually, I *am* a full-time missionary, just in the course of living my life. *(Pointedly.)* You don't have to leave the country to do that, you know.

VOICE: Is that right?

PERSON 3: *(Earnestly.)* I always thought that missionaries were based overseas. But some of the missionaries I sponsor work right here in town. When you think about it, we're *all* missionaries in the sight of God.

VOICE: *(Agreeing politely.)* That *is* interesting.

PERSON 3: Wait! Do you know that I have friends who are missionaries from other countries?

VOICE: *(Politely.)* Do you?

PERSON 3: Yes! They're from England, and they work in the United States! *(Beat.)* Isn't that wild?

VOICE: What's so unusual about that?

PERSON 3: Well, we're always talking about the heathen nations and the third world countries who've never heard of Jesus before. But other countries in the world send missionaries to *America*! In their eyes, *America* is the heathen nation!

VOICE: So you're saying that being a heathen nation is in the eye of the beholder?

PERSON 3: It's subjective, right. But it underscores the point that there's a need for missionaries anywhere…Everywhere!

VOICE: Again, thanks for your time.

PERSON 3: You bet! Don't mention it!

END

Bedtime Story

THEME: Christmas.

DRAMA SUMMARY: A family reads the Night Before Christmas, sort of.

CHARACTERS:

FATHER

MOTHER

CHILDREN

SETTING: A living room.

SCENE: The CHILDREN are lying on the floor in their winter paja-
mas, coloring. The FATHER sits on the couch, quietly reading. The
MOTHER enters, carrying two coffee mugs, which she sets on the table.

MOTHER: Kids, it's time for bed.

CHILD 1 *(Groaning.)* Oh, Mom…

CHILD 2: *(Pleading.)* Can't we stay up a little longer?

MOTHER: *(Giving in.)* Well…

CHILD 3: *(Protesting.)* We haven't had our story yet.

CHILD 1: *(Turning to the FATHER.)* Daddy, will you read us a story?

CHILD 2: *(Begging.)* Please, Dad?

FATHER: *(Giving in.)* Just one story. *(CHILDREN cheer.)* Now gather
around…

(The CHILDREN snuggle with the MOTHER on the couch, as the
FATHER stands and enacts the following story dramatically.)

Twas the night before Christmas when all through the house

Not a creature was stirring, not even a mouse

The children were nestled all snug in their beds

And the joy of salvation danced in their heads.

And my wife in her nightgown and I in my cap

Were settling down for a long winter's nap

When down in my heart there arose such a clatter

I began pacing the floor to see what was the matter.

I saw in the mirror as I was turning around
A glimpse in the darkness; my sins made no sound
They were colored in gray from my head to my foot
All wrinkled and clinging like ashes and soot.

My shoulders were hunched from the weight on my back
And my fist was clenched tightly for greater impact
My anger how bitter, my strife how onerous
I was impure, immoral, dissenting and envious.

I was jealous and cross and viewed others below
And boasted factions and enemies from a long time ago
I didn't like what I saw, it was petty and mean
And didn't seem right to have God's love between

My heart and my mind and all of that clutter
I needed to purge it and close fast the shutter
I chose to give my life over to God
I accepted my Savior with a cry and a nod.

To the window of life I flew like a flash
I opened the curtains and threw up the sash
I'd had a strong feeling my life was amiss
I still hoped to find some metamorphosis.

And what to my wondering eyes should appear
But the fruits of the spirit I no longer feared
More rapid than eagles God's gifts they all came
And I pondered them dear and called them by name.

Now Goodness, Now Kindness, now Self Control and Gentleness
On Faithful, on Peaceful, on Joyful and Patience
In the depths of my heart I heard the gifts call
Now convey everyday, everyway, all.

It's a joyous conclusion, I'm happy to say
That He is my Savior on this wonderful day
My Redeemer, Jesus Christ, the King of Kings
Emmanuel, Prince of Peace, Lord of Everything.

For Christmas is a season to focus on giving
Christ's love in all glory, faithful and forgiving
And I am moved to proclaim as I ponder this sight
Glory Hallelujah to all and to all a good night!

END

Benny And Sheila And Their Warriors Within

THEME: Courage.

SCRIPTURAL REFERENCE: "He gives strength to the weary and increases the power of the weak." *Isaiah 40:29.*

DRAMA SUMMARY: Two meek employees stand up to their supervisor.

CHARACTERS:

BENNY, a shy worker

SHEILA, Benny's meek friend and co-worker

JOSH, Benny and Sheila's abusive supervisor

SETTING: An office.

SCENE: BENNY and SHEILA have been employees in the Accounting Department at the same company for 20 years. They are both plain people who have settled comfortably into middle age. Their costumes are nondescript, and while both are pleasant, their temperaments are meek and shy.

BENNY and SHEILA enter and begin working at their desks. BENNY is on the phone, talking to a customer.

BENNY: *(On the phone.)* Your cost center number will be 29867, and we'll credit your account with that adjustment. Have a good day now!

SHEILA: *(Looks up and spots JOSH walking up the aisle. She warns BENNY frantically.)* Benny! It's Josh!

BENNY: *(Alarmed, covering the phone with his hand and whispering back to SHEILA.)* I thought today was his day off!

SHEILA: Apparently he decided to stop by for his daily torment.

BENNY: *(Dismayed.)* Oh…And the day had started off so well, Sheila.

SHEILA: *(Determined.)* Someday, I'm going to stand up to him.

BENNY: I say the same thing every morning.

SHEILA: *(Glumly.)* We're such cowards, aren't we?

BENNY: *(Switching back to the phone.)* Thanks for holding, Lisa. Yes, I straightened out that account. Let me know if you have any more problems. *(Beat, brightly.)* You're very welcome! Bye bye, now.

(JOSH enters and stands directly behind BENNY.)

JOSH: *(Bellowing in his ear.)* BENNY!

BENNY: *(Startled, he shrieks and drops the phone.)* Oh, hello, Josh. *(Nervously.)* Say, isn't today your day off?

JOSH: What would make you ask that, Benny? Were you planning some sort of subversive activity *behind my back?*

BENNY: N-n-no, not at all. It's such a nice, sunny day, that's all. Today's the kind of day you'd want to spend outside.

JOSH: What's the matter? Being in here's not good enough for you?

BENNY: Th-That's not what I said. I was merely commenting on the lovely weather.

JOSH: I know your type, Benny. You're never grateful for what you have. *(He walks away, then turns back abruptly and coldly.)* If you ever speak to me in that manner again, I'm going to fire you. *(He walks away. BENNY is shocked.)*

BENNY: *(Shocked)* What did I say?

SHEILA: *(Shrugging.)* You *spoke.*

BENNY: I've worked here for 20 years. Doesn't that count for something?

SHEILA: Apparently not.

BENNY: He really could do it, couldn't he? He could just wipe out 20 years of my life because he didn't like the tone of my voice…he simply didn't like the way I looked at him.

SHEILA: *(Agreeing.)* Life isn't always fair.

JOSH: *(He returns suddenly, startling them.)* SHEILA!

SHEILA: *(Screams and drops the file folder of papers she is holding.)* Oh! You startled me!

JOSH: What's the matter with you? You can't hold on to a simple object? I'm surprised you don't drag your knuckles on the ground when you walk.

(SHEILA kneels, picking up what she dropped, in tears.)

JOSH: *(Mocking SHEILA.)* Oh, now she's going to cryyy!

BENNY: *(Looking at SHEILA with compassion, he speaks sharply to JOSH.)* Stop it.

(JOSH makes exaggerated sobbing noises. BENNY has had enough. He stands in front of JOSH and confronts him.)

BENNY: *(To JOSH.)* What is wrong with you?

JOSH: Benny! Poor, pathetic, *unemployed* Benny. *(Evenly.)* Don't be stupid, pal.

BENNY: *(Courageously.)* You know, your threats just don't hold water anymore, Josh. Do you think for one minute that there isn't another employer on the face of the earth—even on this *block*—who wouldn't jump at the chance to hire a hard-working, decent person like me?

SHEILA: *(Sniffling, she stands up and holds her ground, quavering.)* If Benny goes, I go.

JOSH: *(He thinks they're bluffing but is starting to get worried.)* Oh, stop sniveling. Nobody's going anywhere.

SHEILA: *(In a very calm, dignified fashion.)* You think I'm bluffing. I've tolerated your degrading comments and abominable behavior towards Benny and me for far too long. That was my mistake; I take full blame for that. For some deluded reason, I thought I was being polite but all I was doing was enabling you to take advantage of me. And if you think I'm going to remain here and allow it to continue for one more minute, well, then you are very foolish, sir. *(She opens a desk drawer and pulls out her purse, then slams the drawer shut.)*

BENNY: *(Picking up a plant and a framed picture from the desktop and taking it with him.)* You think you're powerful, Josh, but that's only because you pick on people you think are weak. *(Straightening himself proudly.)* Well, as you can see, Sheila and I are more than capable of standing up for ourselves, thank you very much. *(He keys a number into the telephone as if coding the paging system, turns the phone sideways and says, as if announcing into a loudspeaker)* The Accounting

Department is closed! *(JOSH looks up, as if he is hearing this over the loudspeaker.)*

(With dignity, BENNY and SHEILA exit up the center aisle through the congregation. Several phones begin to ring. JOSH stands there dumbfounded.)

JOSH: Benny! Sheila! Wait! *(Beat.)* I was just kidding!

END

The Sex Talk

THEME: Marital communication.

SCRIPTURAL REFERENCE: "Listen to advice and accept instruction, and in the end you will be wise." *Proverbs 19:20.*

DRAMA SUMMARY: Couple seeks marital counseling to improve their sex life.

CHARACTERS:

KEN and NORMA, a couple celebrating their 20th wedding anniversary

RACHEL, the marriage counselor

SETTING: The Counselor's Office.

AUTHOR'S NOTES: *The Sex Talk* was written for an Egalitarians for Biblical Marriage organization seminar.

SCENE: *RACHEL enters and sits in a chair, pulling out a notepad. NORMA and KEN enter and sit on the couch. RACHEL begins taking notes.*

RACHEL: So Norma, when did you first notice these feelings of sexual dissatisfaction?

NORMA: I think it was when my sister got married. She and her husband are very affectionate, and I realized that Ken and I don't seem to have that kind of passion anymore.

RACHEL: And why do you think that is?

NORMA: Well, Ken and I don't spend as much time together as we used to. At least, not as much as a normal couple.

KEN: *(Interjecting defensively.)* Define "normal."

RACHEL: That's a good point, Ken. The term "normal" can be subjective in the context of discussing relationships. What's another good descriptive we can use?

NORMA: How about "healthy"?

KEN: *(Agreeing.)* "Healthy" is good.

RACHEL: In a healthy relationship, both people can say what they need. It's important to be able to negotiate a plan that allows both sides to prioritize and satisfy at least some of those needs.

NORMA: *(Doubtfully.)* Negotiate? That seems a little harsh.

RACHEL: Saying what you need is not unreasonable. That doesn't mean you're going to get what you want but isn't it better to set honest expectations at the start? Why make your partner jump through hoops to guess?

KEN: That makes sense.

RACHEL: Let's go back to your original statement, Norma. Give us an example of a situation where you feel your time together is lacking.

NORMA: Well, I was reading this study that talks about how often a typical couple has sex. Ken and I are beneath the statistical average, both in frequency and duration.

RACHEL: And do you feel pressure to compare your marriage to statistical averages?

NORMA: Of course! *(Complaining.)* Everywhere I turn, there's another survey!

KEN: *(Explaining.)* Norma is always taking those quizzes in the women's magazines.

NORMA: And how do you feel about that, Ken?

KEN: *(Admitting.)* It makes me nervous. I think the standards are unrealistic.

NORMA: *(To RACHEL.)* Our love life is nothing like Cosmo!

RACHEL: What's your reaction, Ken?

KEN: It's too much pressure. Sometimes I feel like Norma has a notebook and stopwatch and is compulsively keeping track of everything we do.

NORMA: *(Denying this.)* I am not!

KEN: You're more concerned about numbers and statistics. What I miss...what I feel is lacking...is just taking time to care for each other.

RACHEL: And now?

KEN: Lately, when I make any kind of gesture, Norma blows it out of proportion. For example, I gave her a backrub last week. It didn't mean I expected anything in return.

NORMA: *(Remembering.)* I was surprised, that's all.

KEN: You were angry. You acted like I was pressuring you, but I wasn't! I did it because I knew you were tired and thought you would appreciate it.

RACHEL: What's your reaction to what Ken is saying, Norma?

NORMA: *(Admitting)* I do tend to read too much into some things.

RACHEL: Why do you think you do that?

NORMA: Ken doesn't say when something is bothering him, so I have to draw it out. Sometimes that means overanalyzing.

RACHEL: Ken, do you agree with this?

KEN: *(Agreeing.)* I could do a better job communicating.

RACHEL: What about sexual overtures? Ken, how do you let Norma know when you're interested in having sex?

KEN: *(Beat.)* I don't have a *newsletter* if that's what you mean.

NORMA: *(Complaining.)* He expects me to be in the mood whenever he's ready.

KEN: Not necessarily to *be* in the mood but at least be willing to *try* to get in the mood.

NORMA: *(Arguing.)* I can't change gears that fast. I need some advance notice. *(Complaining.)* Ken just...*starts*.

KEN: *(Shrugging.)* Well, *someone* has to show some initiative or we'd be there all day.

RACHEL: You raise an interesting point, Ken, that illustrates one of the many differences between men and women. You see, some men view sexual relations as a physical activity, while some women see it from an emotional perspective. And neither is right or wrong, but it's just a difference that the other needs to respect and accommodate.

NORMA: *(To RACHEL.)* So where does this leave us? *(To KEN, putting her hand on his.)* Because I don't want to give up.

KEN: *(Agreeing.)* No, we're not giving up. *(Beat, he takes her hand and shakes it affectionately.)* We just have to learn to communicate better, that's all.

END

Teamwork

THEME: Taming the Tongue.

SCRIPTURAL REFERENCE: "Likewise the tongue is a small part of the body, but it makes great boasts. Consider what a great forest is set on fire by a small spark." *James 3:5.*

DRAMA SUMMARY: Divisive attitudes are perpetuated among a high school girls' basketball team via the coach's backhanded messages.

CHARACTERS:

MRS. PHILPOT, a science teacher and basketball coach

TAMMY, student

LESLIE, student

BETH, student

SETTING: A classroom.

SCENE: MRS. PHILPOT *projects a judgmental attitude toward others, and it shows in the carelessness of her speech. TAMMY and LESLIE are popular, confident, somewhat-snobbish high school students. BETH is a serious, sensitive girl whose moral outrage gives her courage. BETH holds an ongoing grudge against the popular girls, and their disparaging comments about her cousin humiliate her enough to push her over the edge to sever her relationship with them.*
TAMMY and LESLIE enter and sit in the classroom. MRS. PHILPOT enters, waving a piece of paper and hands a roster to the students.

MRS. PHILPOT: *(Greeting TAMMY and LESLIE.)* Ah, there they are, my star basketball players. *(She looks around.)* Where's Beth? I have this year's roster.

TAMMY: *(Grabbing the roster and scanning it.)* Yes! I'm starting forward!

LESLIE: *(Puzzled.)* We're playing on Tuesday nights now?

MRS. PHILPOT: And I am happy to report that the principal has agreed to provide new uniforms for the team.

TAMMY: *(Excitedly.)* Maybe this year we'll be state champs! We were so close last time!

LESLIE: *(Worriedly.)* As long as you get a "C" in science!

TAMMY: *(Turning to MRS. PHILPOT.)* What do you think, Mrs. Philpot? Am I going to pass your class?

MRS. PHILPOT: *(Smiling.)* Since I'm the Science teacher *and* the basketball coach, girls, what do *you* think?

LESLIE: *(Confidently.)* She'll pass.

TAMMY: *(Shrugging.)* Science just isn't my thing. *(She dribbles a basketball.)*

LESLIE: All the good players are back! *(She reads off the list.)* Jones, Miller, Hagelberger, Brown, Smith…*(Puzzled.)* Who's Jean Allen?

MRS. PHILPOT: *(Carefully.)* Oh, we've agreed to take on a new player this year. Jean Allen. She's Beth's cousin.

(BETH enters with a basketball under her arm. The other characters do not see her.)

TAMMY: *(Doubtfully.)* The girl in the remedial class?

LESLIE: The one who talks funny?

MRS. PHILPOT: *(Distastefully.)* She's a little…slower…than the rest of you but I'm told she likes to play basketball.

TAMMY: *(Anxiously.)* But she'll hold us back! We're in the "A" League now.

LESLIE: *(Protesting.)* Everyone makes fun of her! People will sit in the stands and laugh at us!

MRS. PHILPOT: *(Philosophically.)* There's room for *all* kinds on this team…*(beat, sourly)* according to the principal. *(Insincerely.)* It's not like we have a choice, so let's make the best of it. *(Beat.)* Think of it as a *character-building* exercise for us all.

TAMMY: *(Defiantly.)* I'm not going to play if that freak is going to practice with us!

LESLIE: *(Agreeing.)* She makes me nervous…like she's going to steal something when my back is turned.

BETH: *(Speaking up, annoyed.)* Well, which is it? Is she *slow* or is she a thief? You can't have it both ways, you know.

LESLIE: I'm sure your cousin is very nice.

TAMMY: *(Embarrassed that BETH overheard them.)* It's nothing personal, Beth.

BETH: *(Defensively.)* Of course it is. You don't even know her.

MRS. PHILPOT: *(Calmly.)* Now, Beth, if you just give the girls some time to adjust to the situation, it'll work itself out.

LESLIE: *(Hastily.)* All we're saying is that we want to win. We want to have the best players possible.

BETH: *(Retorting.)* Well, I've seen Jean play, and she's pretty good. I think that's all that should matter.

TAMMY: *(Worriedly.)* But people will laugh!

BETH: *(Retorting.)* Maybe they're laughing at *you.*

MRS. PHILPOT: Beth is right, girls. All that matters is basketball. As it happens, we're mandated by law to permit her to participate in activities with the normal students.

BETH: *(Angrily.)* *Normal* students? You mean the ones who can't get a "C" in science without a little help from their basketball coach-slash-teacher?

MRS. PHILPOT: *(Too brightly.)* Oh, Beth, you know what I mean. *(Patronizingly.)* Jean is *special.* I think it's wonderful that she can take part in some of our activities. And we'll be better people for it.

BETH: *(Dryly.)* The only thing that's special about Jean is her free throw average.

TAMMY: We just want to be sure she'll be comfortable playing with us.

LESLIE: *(Agreeing.)* Right.

MRS. PHILPOT: We wouldn't want her to feel *overwhelmed.* This environment might be more...*competitive* than what she's used to.

BETH: *(Beat.)* I don't want to be a part of this team anymore.

TAMMY: *(Cajoling.)* Oh come on, Beth, we were just kidding around. *(Adding.)* You're our best shooter!

LESLIE: You can't leave!

BETH: *(With finality.)* I've got to go. Jean's waiting for a ride. *(She exits.)*
(MRS. PHILPOT rushes offstage after BETH.)

MRS. PHILPOT: *(Calling.)* Wait, Beth! *(Beat.)* Did I mention the
new uniforms?

END

Tranquility

THEME: Peace.

SCRIPTURAL REFERENCE: "But the wisdom that comes from heaven is first of all pure; then peace-loving, considerate, submissive, full of mercy and good fruit, impartial and sincere." *James 3:17-18.*

DRAMA SUMMARY: Woman is bitter about her life. Angel/Pharmacist uses gardening analogy to encourage her to become a seed grower and a harvester of goodness.

CHARACTERS:

PHARMACIST/ANGEL, wearing a white coat and angel's wings

WOMAN

SETTING: A drugstore pharmacy.

AUTHOR'S NOTES: *Tranquility* is about a tiny pharmacy that used to be at the corner of my street. It closed last year and frankly, I'm not surprised. Every time I went to fill a prescription, Dave (the pharmacist) would pleasantly inform me that he didn't carry that particular medication. Antibiotics? Sorry, no. Antihistamines? Sorry, no. Tylenol with codeine? Sorry, no. Finally, I asked him what he *did* carry, and he said "cough drops and Dramamine."

SCENE: The WOMAN is a fretful type and looks for answers in chemical remedies. The PHARMACIST is an angel. He wears a white Pharmacist's coat and angel wings. (The WOMAN does not notice that he is an angel.) The PHARMACIST enters and stands facing the audience, smiling. He smiles persistently throughout the entire drama, and doesn't appear to do any other work, except to stand there and smile. The WOMAN enters, waving a prescription anxiously.

PHARMACIST: *(Cheerfully.)* Good morning! Can I help you?

WOMAN: *(Handing him her prescription.)* I need some blood pressure medication.

PHARMACIST: *(Apologetically.)* I'm sorry, we don't fill prescription drugs here.

WOMAN: *(Puzzled.)* Isn't this a Pharmacy?

PHARMACIST: Well, it's *God's* Pharmacy. We encourage the use of natural remedies.

WOMAN: Oh, like a health food store. Do you carry vitamins?

PHARMACIST: No, I'm afraid not.

WOMAN: *(Grimacing.)* I should have known.

PHARMACIST: What do you mean?

WOMAN: *She* told me to come here. *(Accusatory.)* She knew perfectly well I'd be wasting my time.

PHARMACIST: *(Not sure whether the WOMAN is speaking to him.)* I'm sorry? Who told you to come here?

WOMAN: My best friend, Laura. Well, she *used* to be my best friend. *(Bitterly.)* She's the reason my blood pressure is so high.

PHARMACIST: *(Politely.)* What does she do that upsets you?

169

WOMAN: *(Exclaiming.)* Everything! She does everything better than me! *(She ticks off her transgressions.)* She looks better than me! She has a better job! She's smarter, nicer, healthier, and happier than me!

PHARMACIST: *(Reasonably.)* And why does that make you angry?

WOMAN: Because everyone loves her! You'd think she was a saint, for crying out loud! The whole world rests at her feet, content.

PHARMACIST: *(Happily.)* It sounds rather nice to me.

WOMAN: *(Sulking.)* Well, it's not. There's this calmness about her that is very weird. *(Paranoid.)* It's like she *knows* something.

PHARMACIST: *(Whispering, confidentially.)* What does she know?

WOMAN: *(Shrugging.)* The secret of life, I guess. *(Venting.)* I wish she'd just go away.

PHARMACIST: Do you mean that?

WOMAN: *(Sighing, frustrated.)* No.

PHARMACIST: So, what is it that's upsetting you, really?

WOMAN: *(Anxiously.)* Everything in my life is completely out of control. Why does Laura have tranquility when all I have is chaos?

PHARMACIST: *(Shrugging.)* I think maybe your friend has discovered that being at peace with God brings her peace in her own life.

WOMAN: *(Quickly.)* How can I get that? *(Sadly.)* I'd give anything for that.

PHARMACIST: Well, how considerate are you toward others? Do you show favoritism to some people? Do you make promises sincerely? Can you honestly say: Today I did the right things…I made the right decisions…I honored my ethics and values?

WOMAN: *(Shaking her head.)* Not really.

PHARMACIST: It sounds like you need peace, too.

WOMAN: But how do I get it?

PHARMACIST: It's an elusive, invisible quality. But a visual reminder will help. *(He hands her a Chia pet.)* Here!

WOMAN: *(Puzzled.)* What's this?

PHARMACIST: It's a Chia pet. You water it daily and voila! It grows alfalfa sprouts!

WOMAN: *(Doubtfully.)* I'm not very good with living things. Every plant I've owned died a painful and violent death.

PHARMACIST: It's very low-maintenance, I promise.

WOMAN: *(Looking at the Chia pet.)* I don't understand. How is a Chia Pet going to give me peace?

PHARMACIST: *(Encouragingly.)* Just keep watering and nurturing it. There's so much good inside you that can grow as fast as the chia. Who knows? Maybe some of that growth will inspire you. Maybe if you can see it growing, it will give you hope. *(Beat.)* Maybe that will help you find peace.

WOMAN: *(Doubtfully.)* I guess I can give it a try.

PHARMACIST: *(Brightly.)* Good luck! *(He gasps, looks at his watch.)* Heavens, is it that late already? I've simply got to fly. *(He turns back to the WOMAN.)* Remember, it likes lots of water and sun. Nurture a peaceful environment! *(He exits, waving.)*

WOMAN: *(Tiptoeing and whispering to the plant.)* I can't wait to show Laura!

END

The Kindness Of Strangers

THEME: God's compassion.

SCRIPTURAL REFERENCE: "The Lord is gracious and righteous; our God is full of compassion." *Psalm 116:5.*

DRAMA SUMMARY: Two families console each other as their children undergo emergency surgery.

CHARACTERS:

AL, husband

SHARON, wife

MATT, Sharon's brother

TERRY, another mother at the hospital

NURSE, in scrubs

SETTING: Hospital waiting room.

SCENE: *AL and SHARON are parents of a young child who has been taken to the hospital for emergency surgery. They sit tensely in a hospital waiting room, holding hands, trying to remain composed by not looking at each other.*
TERRY is a single mother of a young child who has also been rushed to the emergency room. She is alone in another row of chairs, away from them. They are strangers.
SHARON's brother MATT rushes in and hugs SHARON emotionally.

SHARON: *(Acknowledging MATT's arrival.)* Did Mom call you?

MATT: *(He pats AL on the shoulder and sits next to SHARON.)* Yeah. I was on my way home and got a "911" on my pager from Mom. I called her on my cell, and she told me what happened. I came right over.

AL: *(Appreciatively.)* Thanks, Matt. We really appreciate your being here.

MATT: *(To SHARON, worriedly.)* Is he going to be okay?

SHARON: *(Worriedly.)* We don't know. It…it doesn't look so good.

AL: *(Explaining.)* He's still in surgery.

MATT: *(Groaning.)* Oh, man. *(MATT hugs SHARON.)* Do you want me to get you something?

SHARON: *(Shaking her head.)* No.

MATT: *(Restless.)* How long has he been in there?

AL: About an hour.

MATT: *(Helplessly.)* I wish there was something I could do.

SHARON: *(Thinking of something.)* Actually…

MATT: Anything.

SHARON: If you could go to our house and get this stuffed bunny that he likes. It's in his crib.

MATT: *(Nodding, anxious to be useful.)* Of course. Sure.

SHARON: *(Tearfully.)* I know it's silly, but I think just having the bunny with him...*(She composes herself, nodding.)* I think he would like that.

AL: *(To SHARON.)* Do you have your keys?

SHARON: Oh! *(She fishes in her purse and gives him her keys.)* Matt, thank you. *(She hugs him.)*

MATT: I'll be back in half an hour. *(He starts to exit.)* You guys, it's going to be okay.

(MATT exits. SHARON and AL resume their silence, not looking at each other. TERRY catches SHARON's eye, and they nod briefly at each other in acknowledgment.)

TERRY: *(Pulling a stuffed bunny from her bag and showing her.)* My daughter has a bunny she likes, too.

SHARON: My son has had his since he was a baby. He won't let go long enough for me to wash it.

TERRY: *(Beat.)* Is your son in surgery? *(SHARON nods.)* So is my daughter.

AL: How long have you been here?

TERRY: It's been about four hours now.

SHARON: Oh! *(She gets up and goes to sit next to TERRY, patting her arm sympathetically.)* Can I get you something?

TERRY: *(Smiling.)* No, it's okay. *(Beat.)* It wasn't supposed to take this long.

AL: *(Agreeing.)* I know. Every minute is agony out here. I just wish we knew something.

(A NURSE in scrubs walks through. They perk up, watching her tensely, wondering if she has news for them. She passes by without speaking.)

TERRY: *(Sliding back down in her chair, anguished.)* Oh! I'm going out of my mind!

SHARON: Are you here by yourself?

TERRY: *(Nods.)* I called my sister, but I couldn't get a hold of her. I left a message on her answering machine.

AL: We've got a cell phone, if you want to use it.

TERRY: Thank you.

(Beat.)

SHARON: *(Worriedly.)* I hope they let me in before he wakes up. He'll be scared if I'm not there.

TERRY: *(Nodding.)* My daughter is three. She's so independent now; she won't even let me put her shoes on. But if I'm not there when she wakes up from her nap, the world ends.

AL: Our son is four. He just started pre-school.

(They chatter aimlessly, trying to distract themselves.)

TERRY: Which pre-school?

SHARON: Harding.

TERRY: That's supposed to be good.

AL: The teacher/child ratio is very low. And they have all kinds of field trips and activities. We've been very pleased.

SHARON: They've got a great soccer team, too. They went to the state championships last year.

TERRY: *(Surprised.)* They have a state championship for *pre-school?*

AL: *(Rolling his eyes in amusement.)* Do you believe it?

(They laugh, then fall silent again.)

TERRY: *(Emotionally.)* I don't know what I'll do if she dies. She's everything to me. *(SHARON covers her mouth, stands up and walks away, the reality of the situation hitting her hard.)*

AL: Don't...don't say that. *(Speaking to both TERRY and SHARON.)* It's just really important to think positively right now.

(The NURSE enters.)

NURSE: Terry?

TERRY: Yes?

NURSE: The surgeon wants to talk to you. We're going in this room over here. *(She points offstage.)*

TERRY: *(Terrified.)* Where is my daughter?

NURSE: She's in the recovery room right now, and we'll be moving her to a room soon. *(She exits.)*

TERRY: *(Relieved, she hastily dabs at her eyes.)* Oh! *(She gathers up her things and begins to rush after the nurse, then stops and turns to AL and SHARON.)* I'll be praying for your little boy. *(AL and SHARON nod appreciatively.)*

SHARON: *(Sincerely.)* Thank you.

AL: *(Waving her off.)* Go, go. *(SHARON and AL stand, hugging each other. They do not face TERRY.)*

(TERRY begins to walk off, then turns back. She takes the stuffed bunny from her bag, looks at it for a moment, and then—unseen by AL and SHARON—walks over and puts it in SHARON's bag.)

END

The Third Denial

THEME: Denial.

DRAMA SUMMARY: Corporate layoffs illustrate self-preservation and denial, without pre-meditated malice.

SCRIPTURAL REFERENCE: Peter replied, "Man, I don't know what you're talking about!" Just as he was speaking, the rooster crowed. The Lord turned and looked straight at Peter. Then Peter remembered the words the Lord had spoken to him. "Before the rooster crows today, you will disown me three times." *Luke 22:60.*

CHARACTERS:

MICHAEL, a supervisor

TOM, an employee

BERT, a Human Resources representative

SARA, an Executive Vice President

SETTING: A Corporate office environment during a layoff.

SCENE: MICHAEL and TOM enter. MICHAEL is slightly older. They play golf and basketball together. They are friends but do not share equal weight in the relationship (i.e., TOM is slightly deferential to MICHAEL, his supervisor). TOM also values MICHAEL's opinion more and tries to emulate him. MICHAEL and TOM are dressed in business attire.

TOM: *(Anxiously ticking off the details.)* I heard Round One is *downstairs*. Everyone else goes *upstairs*. Then the Executive Committee is going to make a second round of cuts before the end of the day.

MICHAEL: *(Reassuringly.)* Tom, they're not going to lay you off. I would never let that happen. You're essential to my team.

TOM: Ever since I challenged the Department Head at the offsite meeting, he's been out to get me. *(With certainty.)* It's a done deal, Michael. My name is on that list.

MICHAEL: *(Reassuring him.)* Everyone is afraid that they're going to get the ax. I still worry, and this is my fourth RIF *(pronounced "Riff")* now.

TOM: *(Looking at MICHAEL blankly.)* RIF?

MICHAEL: "Reduction in Force." *(Reassuringly.)* Trust me. Project Eleven is the highest priority initiative in the company. If you go, my whole team goes.

TOM: *(Disagreeing.)* No, this is personal. I'm telling you, the Department Head wants me out.

MICHAEL: You've been on this project for five years. I promise I'll stand up for you. *(BERT enters from stage right with a clipboard.)* Give me some credit.

BERT: Tom Conway? *(TOM nods.)* Can you come with me?

TOM: *(Gesturing with his thumb.)* I'll just go with Michael.

BERT: *(Awkwardly.)* Sorry—HR policy. Everyone gets escorted to the meeting.

MICHAEL: *(Nudging him.)* Go on. I'm right behind you.

TOM: *(Shrugging.)* Well, okay. *(He starts to walk to stage right.)*

BERT: Um, this way. *(He points to stage left. TOM looks at BERT, and then looks at stage left.*

(Beat. TOM and MICHAEL realize that TOM is being laid off.)

TOM: *(Beat.)* We're going *downstairs*? *(Beat.)* Isn't that where the layoffs are?

BERT: *(Evading the question.)* Um, if you could follow me.

TOM: *(Turning back to MICHAEL questioningly.)* Michael?

MICHAEL: (Waving his hands reassuringly, then points to stage right.) I'm going to straighten this out right now.

(TOM and BERT exit, and SARA enters in time to see TOM departing. MICHAEL turns quickly to go upstairs and runs into SARA. MICHAEL recognizes her as a high-level executive and responds to her professionally and courteously.)

SARA: *(She shakes his hand briskly, introducing herself.)* Sara McLaughlin, Executive Committee.

MICHAEL: Yes, I know. I'm Michael Green in Operations.

SARA: *(Pointing to where TOM exited, in realization.)* Wasn't that the man from the offsite meeting? You know, the project guy who had the meltdown? *(She doesn't wait for an answer, shaking her head, musing.)* Walking pink slip, wasn't he? Too bad his team is going down with him. *(MICHAEL reacts, realizing that his own job may be in jeopardy because of TOM. SARA turns her scrutiny abruptly to MICHAEL.)* He was in Operations, wasn't he? Did you know him?

(TOM re-enters, carrying a banker's box with his belongings and hears MICHAEL's denials. MICHAEL's back is to TOM.)

MICHAEL: Who? *(Gesturing to where TOM exited.)* That guy? *(He shrugs offhandedly, but he is afraid.)* No, no, I didn't know him.

SARA: *(Trying to remember where she knows his name from.)* Michael Green...Aren't you the Team Lead for Project Eleven?

MICHAEL: *(Beat, he is lying. Stronger denial.)* No. No, I'm not.

SARA: Good thing...*(Confiding.)* I just came from the meeting *upstairs*, and Project Eleven was just RIF'd. *(She scrutinizes him again.)* Still, your face looks familiar...I could have sworn you were sitting with him at the offsite.

MICHAEL: *(Stronger denial.)* I told you. I don't know him!

SARA: *(Looking toward stage left.)* So sad, isn't it? *(Sighing, she shrugs.)* Still, better them than us. *(She exits.)*

(MICHAEL turns and sees TOM. Long pause. TOM turns away and exits, as MICHAEL watches, confused by his willingness to sell out TOM under pressure.)

END

Bibliography

Moore, Clement Clarke, *A Visit From St. Nick (Twas the Night Before Christmas)*. 1822.

0-595-19986-0

Printed in the United States
1342700007B/244-246